THE
GREAT
LOBSTER
WAR

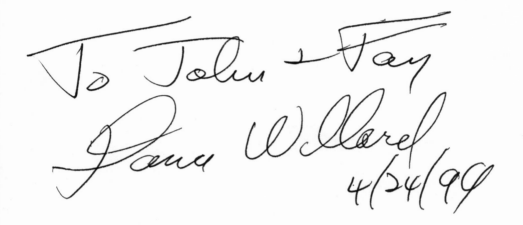

To John + Fay
Dana Willard
4/24/99

Memorial to "The Maine lobsterman," Bailey Island. Elroy Johnson served as the model. Photo courtesy of John Chiquoine.

THE GREAT LOBSTER WAR

RON FORMISANO

University of Massachusetts Press

Amherst

Copyright © 1997 by
Ron Formisano
All rights reserved
Printed in the United States of America
LC 96-8812
ISBN 1-55849-052-3 (cloth); 071-x (pbk.)
Designed by Sally Nichols
Set in Melior
Printed and bound by Braun-Brumfield, Inc.
Library of Congress Cataloging-in-Publication Data

Formisano, Ronald P., date.
        The great lobster war / Ron Formisano.
            p.   cm.
        Includes index.
            ISBN 1-55849-052-3 (cloth : alk. paper). —
    ISBN 1-55849-071-x (pbk. : alk. paper)
            1. Maine Lobstermen's Association—Trials, litigation, etc.
    2. Trials (Conspiracy)—Maine—Portland. 3. Lobster fisheries—Law
    and legislation—United States. 4. Antitrust law—United States.
    I. Title.
    KF224.M235F67   1997
    338.8'363954'09741—dc20   96-8812
                                                                  CIP

British Library Cataloguing in Publication data are available.

This book is published with the support and cooperation of the
University of Massachusetts, Boston.

For
Laura, Matthew
islanders
the island

Contents

THE
GREAT
LOBSTER
WAR

INTRODUCTION

Although this book is about lobster fishermen on the Maine coast, the impulse to write it came to me fifteen years ago while waiting in a "grain line" in the middle of Kansas, a spot near the center of the continental United States, a good place to reflect on the power and contradictions of American individualism. Deep in the heartland, I was sitting in the driver's seat of a 450-bushel wheat truck on a hot summer day during the feverish work of the annual wheat harvest. A grain line forms when the towering cylindrical storage bins known as grain elevators get filled to capacity and trucks, coming in from all over the countryside to unload wheat, queue up in a long train while grain is off-loaded from the elevators into strings of railway cars or monster semitrailers. While waiting, I was fascinated by the wide variety of vehicles streaming to the same place, from pickups and towed wooden wagons (whose cargoes were dumped by raising their front ends in a sling) to big rigs with automatic lifts for dumping. The assortment of trucks seemed to symbolize farmers' historic individualism which, though limited by minimalist cooperative arrangements and by

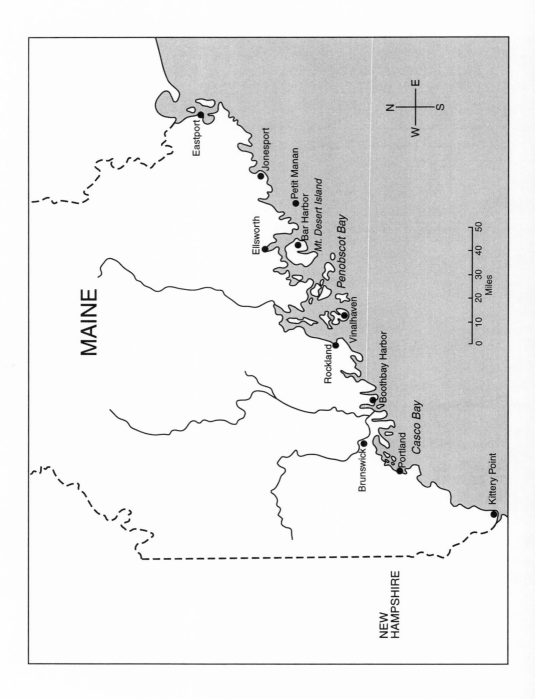

periodic attempts to unite against middlemen and market managers near and abroad, ultimately endured.

A blast of heat and dust from a passing car turned my mind to the evergreen, ever blue, ever cool Maine coast, where as an adult I have always preferred to be in the summer. Suddenly I thought of how much these wheat farmers resembled Maine's lobster fishermen half a continent and a world away. Although lobstermen, or lobstercatchers as many prefer to be known, appear to be more like hunters (and some few have always behaved like predators), they also have been described with some accuracy as farmers of the sea.

The Kansas grain line, and the promptings of an old Maine friend who had experienced firsthand what I call the "Great Lobster War," led me to investigate some extraordinary events that took place along the Maine coastline and in a Portland courtroom more than a generation ago.

In the 1950s Maine lobster fishermen attempted to organize an association that could bargain with wholesale fish dealers to set prices for live lobsters. This action broke with a generations-old tradition

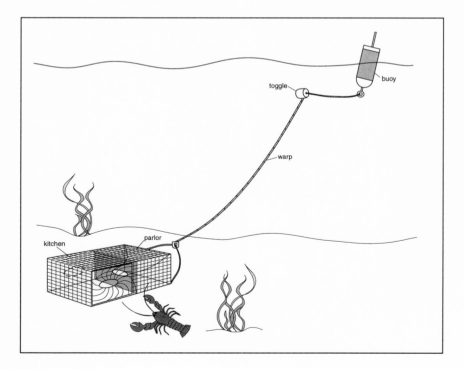

by which dealers, allegedly obeying only the impersonal laws of the market, quoted the daily price at boatside or wharfside to the lobster-catchers. During the summers of 1956 and 1957, as prices typically spiraled down during "shedder" season, when new-shell lobsters are hungry and the catch is large but highly perishable, the fishermen launched two work stoppages or strikes ("tie-ups," the fishermen called them). Some four thousand men, perhaps three-fourths of all Maine's lobstermen, stayed in. Before long, though, the U.S. government charged the lobstermen with conspiracy to violate the Sherman Antitrust Act. A team of Justice Department lawyers from New York City came to Portland to prosecute the Maine Lobsterman's Association (MLA) and its president, Leslie Dyer, a fisherman from the offshore island of Vinalhaven. This story is a drama of charm, humor, and irony, about a group whose values are both strongly and explicitly individualist, and yet also deeply, but implicitly, cooperative and communal. It is ultimately a story about how American individualism gives men who treasure independence a degree of freedom, but at the same time limits their power to control their lives and renders them dependent on others. In short, it is a story that throws into sharp relief the contradictions often inherent in individualism.

To understand why the attempt to organize a lobstermen's association was extraordinary, consider the following joke fishermen tell on themselves. Two lobstermen are out in a thick fog, without radar or compass. Older to younger: "Do you know any prayers?" Yes. "Start praying." The younger man starts praying fervently. The older man: "Not too much, we don't want to be beholden."

The MLA was quite different from the small marketing cooperatives that had engaged small groups of lobstermen along the Maine coast since the late 1940s. The idea for it grew out of years of conversation among men sitting in "liars' chairs" on many wharves, but two unlikely friends brought it to life. Leslie Dyer, a fisherman and local wise man from Vinalhaven Island off Penobscot Bay, and his friend Alan Grossman, a lawyer and Jewish community leader from the nearby midcoast town of Rockland. It was Dyer who sat in the defendant's chair in Portland's federal courthouse in May 1958, pipe in hand accenting his professorial demeanor. And defending him was Grossman, a small-town Clarence Darrow, a short, roundish man with mustache and bow tie, bouncing up with objections to bedevil the squad of government lawyers from the New York office of the Department of Justice—all city folk "from away," as they say in Maine. Dyer, Grossman, and their fishermen allies along the coast had wanted to change fundamentally the way fishermen did business. At the same time, the MLA genuinely wanted to cooperate with dealers to advance the industry's political interests and to develop new marketing strategies. But on the matter of price, they wanted to bargain with buyers as equals. Their stubborn determination to set a minimum price drew the battle line and put them on a collision course with wholesale dealers and eventually with the U.S. government.

Using the work of anthropologists, historians, and others who have written about the lobster fishery, I have tried to locate the MLA within the history and culture of lobsterfishing in Maine. The tie-ups of 1956 and 1957 were in a sense an attempt to overcome the burden of a culture originally steeped in clientage and dependency, traces of which persisted intermittently long after the development of "free labor."* The history of the New England fisheries generally has been characterized by a pattern in which men whose hands controlled capital and markets dominated those men whose hands did the labor. The grand jury hearings, indictment, and trial of Dyer and the MLA constituted an effort to maintain the status quo.

The trial itself forms the largest part of the story told here. The government brought in many fishermen as witnesses, not only to testify concerning the MLA's efforts at price-fixing, but also to substantiate the dealers' charges that the MLA had threatened dissenting fishermen with personal violence or with violence to their boats or gear, and that trap-cutting, a common tactic among feuding lobstermen, had occurred often against "scabs." The exchanges between the city-bred government lawyers and the Maine fishermen constitute by far the most vivid and often most humorous parts of this story. They also reveal a clash between two cultures: one urban and rationalist, the other coastal and commonsensical.

---

* Daniel Vickers, *Farmers & Fishermen: Two Centuries of Work in Essex County, Massachusetts, 1630–1830* (Chapel Hill, 1994), provides a broad historical perspective on the economics of fishing in New England.

On the witness stand, some fishermen—the MLA loyalists— engaged in protracted struggle with their interrogators. Other fishermen witnesses were simply frightened or befuddled. Of course, many persons in Maine and elsewhere could not understand why the government was prosecuting a group of such quintessentially small businessmen for violating the Sherman Antitrust Act, passed by Congress originally to foster economic competition through regulation of giant national corporations.

Although the federal government had entered the picture at the request of a Portland lobster dealer, the grand jury hearings had culminated in separate indictments of the fishermen and, surprisingly, of several dealers (also on charges of price-fixing). The proceedings against the dealers will make up only a small part of the story told here. Their importance for the lobstermen's trial lay primarily in the judge's not allowing the defense to argue that the lobstermen's actions were a response to prior conspiracy by the dealers. That ruling, though it attracted little notice from observers at the time, would be the axis on which the trial turned.

The presiding judge, Edward Gignoux, tall and Lincolnesque in a handsome way and blessed with a deep, rich voice, looked and sounded as if he had come from central casting in Hollywood. He had just been appointed to the federal bench and was the youngest person yet to have been so honored in U.S. history. Gignoux, an icon of the local establishment, impressed both sides with his fairness and good sense. Moreover, he knew the coast and appreciated the tangle of miscommunication that often arose between fishermen and lawyers during the trial. He would be fondly remembered by the parties to this legal struggle—even by the losers.

The defense lawyers were all that was Maine, yet remarkable for their cultural diversity. Grossman, now far from the Jewish neighborhood in Dorchester, a sprawling section of Boston, with his young, diminutive, but scrappy Irish-Catholic junior partner, John Knight, from Rockland, a coastal town with a working harbor and few tourist frills, was joined by Stanley Tupper, a tall, cool Yankee Episcopalian from picturesque Boothbay Harbor. One handsome fishermen called as a witness so much looked his part that he had served as a model for statues of "The Maine Lobsterman" that still grace a public square in

Portland and a peninsula known as Land's End on Bailey Island. The government team was headed by an urbane Irish-Catholic who had grown up in Cambridge, Massachusetts, and was rumored to have a taste for fresh seafood. His associates included one New Yorker, one Bostonian, and a rural Arkansan, all of whom regarded Maine as a foreign country. But they all welcomed the case, according to local attorneys, because a successful prosecution would look good in their dossiers.

Public sympathy, of course, heavily favored the fishermen, as did press coverage. In court, the fishermen and Alan Grossman seemed on most days to have gotten the better of the government "highlanders," whose ignorance of nautical terms and local dialect produced frequent merriment. Though he did not take the stand, Leslie Dyer was an enormously charismatic presence, adored by the fishermen and respected even by the men prosecuting him. When rumors flew that he might be fined $50,000, reporters gleefully quoted his terse rejoinder: "If I had $50,000 I'd be worried."

Five years before the trial, another pronouncement became part of the Dyer legend. "A fisherman is an independent as a hog on ice, and twice as ornery." In the early stages of research for this book, talking to Casco Bay folk about the trial, I heard that sentence often. What I later discovered, however, was that Dyer, testifying to a legislative committee about a gauge increase, actually said: "We fishermen in Maine are as independent as a hog on ice—*and just as helpless.* We're more or less set in our ways and we don't like to be dictated to." But it was the helplessness that selective memory excised, revealing unintentionally the transforming power of the mystique of lobsterfishing individualism.

Longtime inhabitants of Casco Bay—where the tie-ups of 1956–57 originated—boast that the bay's waters contain 365 islands, called the "Calendar Islands." The number of islands is calculated by defining an island as any place a man can stand at high tide without getting wet. Though the claim may be exaggerated, it hints dramatically at the stark individualism of the region's inhabitants.

And among Mainers, lobstermen supremely enjoy the image of fierce individualists. On any day, they decide for themselves whether to work or not, they are their own bosses. The shape of their sloop-hulled vessels alone makes a statement of competence, each one self-sufficient, contained, a small workshop, a miniature factory, a floating artisan culture. Like those small farmers who still somehow manage to survive in the late twentieth century, the lobster fisherman must be part mechanic, part businessman, and part naturalist. Who can deny the appeal of the fresh sea air on those sparkling blue, white, and golden early mornings, working alone except for gulls wheeling overhead, on a calm sea under a brilliant sun? Outsiders, taken with the romantic image, do not understand that such individualism comes at a price. And for reasons intimately connected to competition and secrecy among themselves, fishermen have skillfully managed to perpetuate their reputation as individualists, especially to outsiders. Though partly a product of impression management, their image is not false, but it masks a deeper complexity consisting of webs of dependency on one another. More vitally it hides a lack of autonomy, of independence, of power, at the most crucial point of their economic life. Many thoughtful fishermen wish it were otherwise, but in a real sense they are prisoners of individualism, both its image and its reality. Living partly within the confines of an illusion that proclaims their superior independence to the land- and office-locked average citizen, lobstermen may not be so different from many others of their fellow countrymen.

1 MOORINGS

here are few things more graceful than a Maine lobster boat with a curl of blue and white water at its prow. The hull's profile announces its descent from the sailing sloops first used for commercial lobstercatching in the early 1800s, and its broad beam steadies a working platform for hard and sometimes dangerous work. Harmonious blends of form and function, Maine lobster boats cut through choppy waters with ease. During the course of a workday, they can crawl steadily as traps are hauled or set (thrown over), they can circle buoys in tight, clean arcs, or they can steam rapidly across open water to new fishing grounds.

On a typical summer day along the Maine coast, at the countless wharves where work and pleasure boats mingle, summer folk clamber awkwardly off floats into their power- or sailboats, and then uncertainly get under way to open water. Meanwhile, a lobster boat slips noiselessly into the dock with balletic precision, its helmsman wearing a mask of nonchalance and handling the *Susan Adams* or *Sea Ghost* or *Old Salty* with almost imperceptible movements. Anyone in the vicinity who might be preoccupied at that moment, not looking, realizes a lobster boat has arrived only by the smell of rancid fish—the tubs of lobster bait on board.

The endless repetition of such scenes has provided only one element of what has gone into creating the image of the lobster fisherman as rugged individualist. The mind's eye of summer people, of course, has helped greatly in casting the fisherman's image into stereotypes. Twenty and thirty years ago caricatures of the lobstermen flourished. Wealthy vacationers at cocktail parties would trade stories about their favorite characters: the strong, silent individualist, a law unto himself; or the wharf eccentric, with his one-liner put-downs of tourists that variously marked him as native wit or simple clown; or the stoic rescuer of unlucky sailors in distress. Some element of truth adheres to each of these types.

The independence of lobster fishermen is real. They can indeed decide for themselves whether to work on a given day; they spend seemingly infinite stretches of time on the water, working alone, or with one helper (a sternman—often now, two sternmen), locked into a rhythm of work that demands full attention. They plan their days around wind, tide, and weather, elements of a nature that can be beneficient and bountiful but also unforgiving and punishing.

For the weather or their work can quickly turn dangerous. Infrequently, but lethally, a fisherman may get tangled in his gear, pulled overboard, and drowned, and not just in bad weather. Engine fires and explosions have killed and maimed others. And when talk turns to competitors who may be deliberately cutting away the buoys marking where a man's traps are located, an implied menace of violent retaliation against gear, boats, or persons inevitably arises. Although rarely, sometimes the talk becomes action and traps are cut away, boats are damaged or, as recently as 1993 in Casco Bay, weapons are brandished and even fired at boats.

All of this is true, yet needs to be qualified not only with additional layers of image and perception but also by other dimensions of reality. Lobster fishermen, for all their apparent laconic indifference to outsiders, are in fact masters of "impression management." That attribute's relationship to summer people and other outsiders is almost incidental, though, because it springs primarily from fishermen's relations with other fishermen and with the buyers and dealers to whom they sell their lobsters week by week, or day by day during the high fishing season of midsummer to early fall.

All generalizations about Maine lobstering must also be weighed against the variations along one of the world's most highly differentiated coastlines. There exist, in fact, several Maine coasts. They begin on the New Hampshire border near Kittery at the south and west (the coast runs more west to east than south to north) with a strip of some forty-five miles of relatively straight, sandy ocean beach ending at Casco Bay and Portland, the state's ancient shipping and commercial capital. Just below the many wharves of Portland, Casco Bay begins at Cape Elizabeth and the shore curves in making a rough half moon ending at Cape Small, a scant twenty nautical miles away.

Within Casco Bay itself the coast has broken already into the many evergreen-crested peninsulas, rocky islands, coves, and inlets that dominate the topography from Small Point to Penobscot Bay, roughly in the middle of the state's coast. Beyond midcoast the water becomes deeper, the rocks, ledges and trees more dramatic, the distances greater, and the fishing ports fewer, reaching "Down East" beyond Mount Desert Island and its famed Bar Harbor another hundred miles to Eastport.

Lobstering in the Down East and midcoast regions still fits classic outlines of myth and mystique. Changes in traditional lobsterfishing mores (not necessarily techniques) have taken hold more slowly Down East. In 1991, for example, an attempt to legislate trap limits (each fisherman could set up to a fixed maximum number) had gained surprising support within the industry, but was defeated by a show of opposition mainly from Down East. The region from Kittery to Casco Bay and just beyond, on the other hand, has been more exposed to tourism, development, and a flood of lobsterfishing newcomers who do not observe, or even know, lobstering traditions.

Casco Bay is also distinctive in its trap-hauling techniques, which have been driven by an almost frenzied entrepreneurial spirit. In the 1930s some Cliff Island fishermen, hearing that lobster catches were enormous off Rhode Island, went to Newport to fish. Returning eventually to Casco Bay, they brought back with them the technique of putting out many traps on a single "string." The result has been a proliferation of traps from Portland to Boothbay but, in the words of an old fisherman, "No trawls [strings] East of Boothbay, no trawls West of Cape Elizabeth. . . . Just singles and pairs." This condition exists not by state law, but by tradition. "They aren't allowed because the fishermen would take them in their own hands. Trawls they would just cut away."

Legend has it that lobsterfishing is a kind of birthright, passed on from one generation to the next. Not only do fathers hand down skills and equipment to their sons, they also bequeath fishing territories that were handed on to them by their fathers. Representatives of such family lines can yet be found across the length of the coast, especially Down East, but were more common in the 1950s than they are now. Even then, legend obscured economic reality for many men who went lobsterfishing at some stage of life or at different periods of their lives, and who did other kinds of fishing for years at a time.

In recent times some men work land-based jobs for most of the year and then fish in the hot months of shedder season: "summer dubbers," as the inept among them have been called. Many part-timers have come and gone, some have fished on and off for decades. Lobstering as a full-time activity does not seem to have developed until the 1930s, when large powerboats and improved traps became available.

Bernard Johnson is a retired lobstercatcher in his late sixties living on Bailey Island in Casco Bay. A short, graying man with a solid and friendly face, he is direct and articulate. In different clothing he could pass for an insurance agent or a fatherly minister. Unlike many fishermen, he is not circumspect or hesitant with strangers. His uncle, Elroy Johnson, was the paragon of lobstercatching who modeled for statues of the generic "Maine Lobsterman." But Bernard Johnson, sidelined now after a heart attack, speaks heretical words about lobstering.

At different times in his life this "lobsterman" worked at dragging, gillnetting, mackerel trapping, and tuna fishing. He enjoyed dragging the most and, though draggermen own a reputation for being less environmentally sensitive, he found draggers to have more espirit de corps and feeling of mutual support than lobsterfishermen. "I didn't care for lobsterin' the way I did draggin'. . . . The challenge isn't there. Draggin' you have to use your head." Lobstering he calls "an everyday thing, like a postman." You could always make money lobstering, but not big money like in dragging. And draggers were more independent.

"Lobstering just takes common sense. You wouldn't put traps where they would disappear in a storm any more than you would park your car on a freeway. Anyone can put a trap anywhere and they would still catch *something*."

In the early 1800s it was even simpler. Lobsters were so plentiful they could be caught by hand or, with less hazard (because the average lobster was so large), with a gaff, a pole with a large hook stuck in the end. More systematic efforts began around 1820 when small sailing vessels called "well smacks" arrived off Maine seeking lobsters for urban markets. The smacks' hulls contained a tank, or "well," through which fresh seawater circulated, permitting portage of live lobsters over long distances. In their superb book *Lobstering and the Maine Coast,** Kenneth R. Martin and Nathan R. Lipfert speculate that the smacks probably introduced Casco Bay to a new catching method: "lobster pots." These semirigid nets, open at the top and shaped like baskets, could be baited, dropped into shoal waters, and raised quickly after the critters crawled in. They required, of course, almost constant tending. Sometime around 1830, however, the "lath trap," which was shaped like a half-cylinder or a rectangle and could be left overnight, spread through Casco Bay. That basic design did not change much for nearly a hundred and fifty years. Only in the 1980s did many lobster-men move away from wooden traps to longer-lasting rectangles made of steel and plastic-coated wire mesh.

In sharp contrast to mid-twentieth-century practice, in the 1830s the heavy fishing season ran from March to July, *before* the shedders swarmed. Thus the early fishery practiced better resource protection, because newly molted lobsters are much more perishable and damage easily. Still, it was an industry for which regulation was slow to develop, and what few checks there were on unrestrained exploitation proved difficult to enforce.

As a lobster-canning industry flourished along the length of the coast from the 1840s to the 1870s, employing some eight hundred persons by 1880, the size of the lobsters caught declined rapidly. Boat-loads of lobsters, large and small, poured through these seaside fac-tories. In 1872 the state of Maine reacted with the first lobster law,

* (Bath, Maine, 1985)

prohibiting the taking of females bearing eggs ("seeded" or "berried" lobsters). Two years later, the state prohibited the taking of lobsters under ten and a half inches overall and closed fishing from August 1 to October 15. Many fishermen ignored these size regulations for a long time, but further restrictions eventually doomed Maine's canning industry. That decline, however, was paralleled by a boom in lobster factories across the border, in Canada's Maritime Provinces.

Meanwhile, in the 1880s and 1890s, a pattern emerged for lobster-fishing that has continued to the present. A price climb after 1880 stimulated more men to fish and to greater effort. The influx brought an 1885 law requiring fishermen's names to be branded onto pot buoys and establishing the first penalties for interfering with another's traps. (Licensing of lobstermen would not become obligatory until 1917.) In 1889 more than 2,000 catchers landed a record 25 million pounds, worth seven and a half cents a pound. But in 1898, with nearly 3,100 catchers, pounds landed fell to 17.5 million even though the number of pots set increased by almost 25 percent.

The cycle has repeated with rhythmic regularity: more catchers, more traps and gear, more overhead, but the same amount of lobsters caught, sometimes less. If prices keep rising, the fishermen are rewarded; usually, though, prices have stabilized for long spells or even declined (as in recent years). All this must be qualified by the fact that official data on pounds landed have not included lobsters sold on the side by lobstermen to vacationers and tourists during the summer months (not to mention those consumed by themselves). For some fishermen, these sales, at prices per pound above the boat price (usually a bargain for the buyer), are significant income and well worth the hassle of dealing with "summer complaints." But for many fishermen, the pressure of rising costs and catch-effort too often makes them think they are just running in place.

At the turn of the century, fishermen began converting many of their sloops, dories, and skiffs to power. By 1910 most Casco Bay fishermen were using powerboats, and within another twenty years the typical lobsterfishing boat had acquired its classic form from Portland to Rockland at the head of Penobscot Bay. Traps had improved also, with the entries having been shifted from opposite ends of the cylinder to facing each other across one half. Thus lobsters now entered a "parlor" at one side and then moved to the bait through an interior entryway leading to the other end of the trap, the "kitchen."

Just after World War I the lobster fishery fell into a prolonged depression with very low production. In the Roaring Twenties, as the middle classes discovered new joys of consumption, lobster prices shot up to an average of 32.1 cents per pound in 1924 while the Maine catch sagged to 5.5 million pounds. Then the Great Depression wiped out consumer purchasing power, prices plummeted, and many lobster-catchers moved to other lines of work.

The depression also spurred changes in size laws. In 1932 no lobster could be taken whose carapace (or "body," measured from the eye sockets to where the tail begins) was under three and a half inches. The next year, that measure became three and one-sixteenth inches, and a legal maximum of four and three-quarters inches was established. Dealers had promoted the latter change, since hard times had made jumbo lobsters a tough sell, and fishermen concerned to protect the breed stock had supported the change.

The booming economy of World War II lifted the lobster industry out of the doldrums. The present fishery may be said still to be an offspring of the war and its impact on American society. The armies of unemployed melted away as the manpower demands of the military resulted in a surge of women, minorities, and even the handicapped into the work force. Military industries paid well, wages climbed, and consumers once again ate out in restaurants and could afford to buy lobsters. The average Maine lobster catch from 1941 to 1945 rose to 17.7 million pounds, and the price to an unprecedented 40.1 cents. Soon the total catch was setting new records for value.

In the 1940s and 1950s many returning veterans found lobstering attractive as a year-round enterprise. Yet the price-effort-and-overhead spiral intensified once again. In 1940, 3,717 licensed lobstercatchers had fished 222,000 traps. By 1955 nearly 6,000 fishermen, with 552,000 traps, were landing 22.8 million pounds, a catch far outweighing 1940 and other lean years, but less than the bumper years of the past. By 1965 catch-effort would double again, but production had leveled off as costs rose. To keep up with competitors the boats needed to be bigger, faster, and equipped with new technology such as fathometers or radar, not to mention carrying more insurance.

Dealers had responded already to the organizational imperative that historically has been quickened by war, and Canadian together with U.S. lobster dealers had formed the North Atlantic Lobster Institute, a trade consortium whose purpose was to improve the fishery and modernize marketing, and, a less publicized but critical objective, to lobby state houses and congressmen for favorable legislation. As fishermen saw dealers pursuing legislation that vitally affected them but without consulting them, they soon followed the dealers' example and organized.

The Maine Lobstermen's Association sprang from a growing distrust among fishermen of the dealers to whom they sold their catch, and supremely from a desire for higher prices. The relationship between fishermen and dealers historically had been ambivalent, charged with tension. In the early 1950s, as fishermen hauled in bumper crops of unprecedented dollar value, they asked why the price paid to them remained low, and wondered out loud where all the cash was going. The answer for many, especially for MLA organizers, was that dealers conspired to fix prices, took more than a reasonable share, and deprived lobstercatchers of a fair return on their labor.

A most unlikely pair of friends created and sustained the MLA: Leslie C. Dyer, a lobsterman from a fishing family on the island of Vinalhaven off Penobscot Bay, and A. Alan Grossman, a Rockland lawyer originally from Boston. Dyer had discussed the possibility of some such organization many times with Grossman and other fishermen for years. The immediate impetus came from a sober Down East group from Beals Island and Jonesport headed by Farrell Lenfesty of Beals, a lobstercatcher and ordained minister in the Reorganized Church of Jesus Christ of Latter-day Saints. Lenfesty's grandfather came to Maine on a square-rigger as an immigrant from the Isle of Guernsey and had taken up farming, but his father had been a lobsterman who had long advocated the need to organize. One day in September 1954 Lenfesty and several other fishermen, after sharing laments about recent damage from two hurricanes, and after absorbing the usual post–Labor Day nosedive in lobster boat-prices, decided to "form a union." So five of them piled into a car and drove a hundred and twenty miles to Rockland to seek advice from Grossman, well known already as a fishermen's advocate.

In Grossman's office they hatched a plan for a statewide organization whose prime purpose was "to combat price fixing by dealers" so that lobstermen could make a "liveable income." "They [dealers] pay 25 cents a pound now," said Lenfesty, "and that isn't a liveable wage." In announcing their plan to the press, Grossman said that he had conferred with Vinalhaven lobstermen about the plan and that they had given it their blessing. Grossman had spoken, of course, with his friend Leslie Dyer, with whom he had appeared at a legislative hearing in Augusta (the state capital) the previous year to testify against a dealer-sponsored bill which would increase the minimum legal length of lobsters. Dyer soon would be elected first president of the Maine Lobstermen's Association and would be reelected yearly over the next decade.

Fifty-six years old in 1954, Dyer was a most unusual fisherman and more than just a politic spokesman for lobstermen. Slight, spectacled, with graying, red-brown hair and a gentle expression on his youthful face, Dyer looked more like a minister or physician. His ever present pipe helped give him an aura of calm reflection, and one of his admirers bestowed on him the title of "Caleb in oilskins," a prophet leading his people to the land of milk and honey. It was a fact that probably no other man was as trusted as Leslie Dyer in so many fishing villages along the length of the coast.

Eventually Dyer wound up wintering in Rockland on Willow Street, a couple of doors down from his friend Alan Grossman, but he was born on spectacularly beautiful Vinalhaven Island, a jagged jigsaw-puzzle piece of rock in the middle of the wide mouth of majestic Penobscot Bay. Vinalhaven, while not as remote as the islands of Monhegan and Matinicus, in the 1950s was not yet served by a state ferry. Though independent and self-sufficient in the manner of island people, its fishermen in the 1930s had begun to organize one of the first cooperatives on the coast, but it apparently never got beyond the planning stage.

Dyer started fishing around 1909, at age eleven, in a small sailing skiff. After graduating from Vinalhaven High School in 1916 he enlisted in the Marines and served through World War I on the USS *Texas*. He was commissioned on discharge as a second lieutenant in the Marine Corps Reserve, and later became a captain in the National

Guard Coast Artillery. But the wanderlust with which wartime travel has intoxicated so many young men had taken hold, and Dyer went back to sea briefly.

Already married to a local woman, Hazel Mae Rogers, Dyer returned to Vinalhaven and to lobsterfishing, and over a sixteen-year period he fathered eight children, two daughters and six sons. Yankee self-improvement proved strong in the Dyer household: three sons attended and two completed studies at the University of Maine, one after Korean War service and another after fishing for ten years. One daughter became a registered nurse; three sons remained in lobsterfishing, one of them becoming also a boat and cottage builder. The youngest daughter, Ada Mae, married a master mechanic on whom island boat-owners and fishermen depended to keep their boats running.

A sense of service to country ran deep in the Dyer family. The day after the Japanese attacked Pearl Harbor, December 8, 1941, Leslie Jr., nineteen, and George Burton Dyer, eighteen, enlisted in the Navy. Phillip would enlist in 1944. Leslie Jr. was hurt in an accident on board ship and came home to resume fishing, now with a wooden leg. The oldest Dyer child, Carolyn, had married an electrician who entered the high-risk ski patrol and was killed. Les Sr. wanted to enlist in the merchant marine to do his part, but Hazel said that sending sons was enough. One of the youngest, Richard, served during the Korean War. Les later became state commander of the Veterans of World War I, and lived to see one of his grandchildren enlist in the Marines.

Before and after the war, Dyer gave his time unstintingly to his community, serving at various times as school committeeman, church trustee, and briefly as town selectman and tax collector in the late 1930s. For many islanders, Les acted as sort of an unofficial ombuds-man. No lawyer lived on Vinalhaven year round then, and though Dyer was self-educated, locals would go to him for legal advice on routine matters, especially those involving deeds and property transfers. There is a picture of Dyer in his prime in the 1939 Rockland *Courier-Gazette:* the newly elected "King Lion" of the Vinalhaven Lions, looking like an earnest deacon with his square chin and sensitive eyes.

Gentle demeanor aside, Dyer's popularity owed as much to his shrewdness and keen sense of humor, which expressed itself usually in the classically understated Maine mode. Dyer could be tart, too, though always in a soft-spoken easy manner. When testifying in 1953 regarding a lobster gauge-increase, he sarcastically agreed with the dealer preceding him who had called the proposal a conservation measure: it would indeed conserve lobsters . . . by putting most fishermen out of business. "The dealers," he said, drawing adroitly upon Cold War anti-Soviet rhetoric, "have set themselves up as a little Politburo to make up their own legislation and cram it down our throats." Dyer was in many ways a populist, at ease sitting down with the governor for a mug of coffee or trading yarns with the boys at the corner store. In taking on the task of organizing the unorganizable, Dyer seems to have been driven by a keen sense of fair play, by a desire to give fishermen some leverage in what can only euphemistically be called "price negotiations."

His partner in that effort was a local lawyer who in some ways was even more remarkable than Dyer. "Caleb's" friend and ally in leading the Yankee fishermen out of the price wilderness, Alan Grossman, was a pillar of Rockland's Adas Yashuron Synagogue. His parents were immigrants from Romania who had run a grocery store in Dorchester, Massachusetts, and who had raised, in the classic Jewish American pattern of upward mobility, five sons and daughters who became professionals. Alan helped in the store after high school and then began attending Suffolk University Law School. In 1937 he married a woman from Maine who he met in Boston, Constance Miller, and after law school the Grossmans decided to settle in her hometown of Rockland.

Constance's grandparents were Russian-Jewish immigrants, and her parents had formed part of a small congregation in Rockland of about twenty families. Alan was aware that for a city-bred, Jewish lawyer this Maine coastal town—where the Ku Klux Klan had marched not so long ago—might not be the most hospitable environment. But he thrived, typifying what Judith Goldstein, in her elegant study of Jewish assimilation in Maine, has characterized as a time of emergence and falling barriers for Jews in a predominantly Protestant society.* While maintaining his Jewishness—he served as president of his synagogue for twenty-five years, and after the late 1940s was deeply concerned

---

* Judith S. Goldstein, *Crossing Lines: Histories of Jews and Gentiles in Three Communities* (New York, 1992).

about the new state of Israel—Alan Grossman served all of Rockland on the school board and also was at home in the thoroughly Gentile local Kiwanis, Masons, Shriners, and Grangers. Unlike his friend Les Dyer, who supported Democrats such as Edmund Muskie for governor, Grossman was a moderate "Eisenhower Republican" in the 1950s and would eventually become judge of probate in his community.

Round-faced, balding, with dark-rimmed glasses and often sporting a small mustache, Alan Grossman established a successful practice in Rockland because he was a hard worker and a quick-witted courtroom lawyer with a flair for the dramatic. "He could really move around that courtroom," recalled an attorney and former rival. "He should have been an actor," said a Rockland newsman. He could shift modes rapidly. He had, said one reporter, "the blankest stare you'd ever want to see." But with a disarmingly cherubic smile he could also "take an inch of hide off a witness before they knew it." Always immaculately dressed and sporting a bow tie, Grossman quickly gained a reputation as a skilled advocate.

He was also tireless in wearing down a witness, once keeping a local policeman on the stand for several hours trying to define the word "drunk." Defending a local businessman against a drunk-driving charge, Grossman told his client, "You're guilty as hell and you're going to pay for getting me to get you off, but don't do it again, because if you do I won't defend you." In 1953 he also took on the defense of a Matinicus Island lobsterman accused of shooting at a rival during a highly publicized trap-cutting war that had gone too far. The Rockland trial resulted in the judge ordering a $1,000 "peace bond" to be posted by the adversaries.

Representing fishermen in trouble was good public relations and good business, but like his friend Les Dyer, Alan Grossman was at heart a populist interested in fair play, and he gave to fishermen's organizations far more than he gained. In June 1955 when herring fishermen, inspired by the lobstermen, decided to organize the Maine Coastal Seiners and Weirmen's Association in Rockland, Grossman of course was there as legal counsel. At their annual meeting in December, the herringmen complained of problems similar to those of lobster fishermen, including bad state and local laws enacted in the name of conservation, and of fish canners exploiting fishermen in times of abundance:

fishermen, the herringmen said, needed to refuse to make sales of fish "not in accordance with the state measure . . . [in order to] break up the evil practice where fisherman is played against fishermen."

Similarly blunt rhetoric had accompanied the first stages of the Maine Lobstermen's Association, but by the time of its official launching, the MLA and Dyer had adopted a more conciliatory tone, and explicit discussion of price was absent from its statement of purposes. Indeed, one of the MLA's objectives, Dyer said, was to create a spirit of cooperation between dealers and lobstermen. "We must have dealers . . . and we expect them to make a reasonable profit. By the same rule, we shall never cease to work for a reasonable profit for the lobstermen. Without lobstermen there would be no lobster dealers."

The MLA sported a lengthy agenda besides a desire to leverage prices. Many of its proposals, it turned out, involved action (and usually spending) by the federal government: establishment of a federal Department of Fisheries; funds for commercial fisheries courses in schools and colleges; long-term loans to boatowners and dealers; government-sponsored studies of various phases of the lobster industry; regulation of lobster-meat imports; state prohibition of hauling traps thirty minutes after sunset and thirty minutes before sunrise. On closer inspection, though, several of these items would have the effect of giving lobstermen leverage on price, in some cases by giving them independent information about markets and prices. Dyer and Grossman were proposing that Uncle Sam study the processing and marketing of lobsters during shedder season, for example, for the simple purpose of providing a yardstick against which to measure dealers' prices.

By August 1955, moreover, even before the MLA's first annual meeting, Grossman and Dyer were anticipating possible conflict with dealers. Prices predictably fell in midsummer, and by late August Dyer was telling newspapers that he advised fishermen to quit hauling until prices rose above the current average of 25 cents. He warned: "If this thing keeps up the dealers may drive us into the marketing business as well as fishing." Dealers replied that floods in Massachusetts and Connecticut had caused many Maine vacationers to cut short their stay and leave for home. Floods also had blocked roads and railroads, preventing shipment of lobsters to city markets.

In October a couple hundred lobstermen, many with their wives, gathered in Rockland for the MLA's convention. Some had proposed making it a typical male convention of the era, a boy's night out, a "hot time" with "lots of booze and show girls," but the Farrell Lenfestys prevailed in setting a more sober tone, at least for the public gatherings (Lenfesty delivered the benediction). Les Dyer promised the enthusiastic crowd that the MLA was here to stay and would not "blow up" like some of its predecessors, though "there are people who want to see it fail." He lost no time in claiming credit for the association in holding prices up that autumn "when the dealers wanted to drop us to 25 cents and even less." He hoped that some day we could set minimum prices below which no one would go if we stuck together, and that as soon as next year "we can base our prices on market reports of what the dealers are getting." As the fishermen left Rockland, they took back with them to towns from Kittery to Eastport the belief that the MLA would be effective in keeping up prices, and this more than anything fueled MLA growth over the next two years.

Grumbling about boat price was probably as old as the lobster fishery itself. When the first smacks sailed out of Casco Bay around 1820 they probably left a good deal of second-guessing in their wake. But the fledgling MLA was challenging a set of arrangements, a culture really, that had existed for generations. World War II had given the lobstermen new prosperity and new status, yet the fundamental relationship between dealers and fishermen remained much the same.

In 1957–58 some 125 dealers and buyers were doing business along the Maine coast. A buyer usually is a small operator who pays cash to fishermen for their daily catch and resells to dealers who operate established wholesaling to restaurants and stores, local and distant. By the late 1940s a belief that the larger dealer-wholesalers were engaged in price-fixing had taken deep root in the minds of many Maine fishermen. Their relationship with those men was at once personal and impersonal, fraught with tension and suspicion, and conducted under an aura of mutual independence that disguised what was often the fisherman's ambivalent dependence on the dealer.

On any given day, a fisherman cannot be sure of the price. He finds out from the dealer, who simply announces that "the price is x." The lobsterman accepts that price or he goes (using fuel) to another dealer, but chances are that any other dealer in the vicinity will offer the same or nearly the same price.

Dealers are reluctant to discuss their practices and pricing with anyone. The code of *omertà* among the Mafia was no more powerful in the 1950s than the pressure of economic competition which sealed the lips of the dealers, who kept their market information to themselves. The author of an obscure 1953 master's thesis at the University of Maine reported driving 152 miles to interview one such dealer regarding prices, coming away with this short sentence: "Lord, dear, I just buy 'em and sell 'em the best way I can." That same student asked ten dealers what percentage of their sales went to retailers, restaurants, and wholesalers: five would not answer.

The anthropologist James Acheson, perhaps the most knowledgeable scholar of the lobster fishery's culture, has written: "The process by which prices are negotiated and changed is deliberately hidden from fishermen. To avoid unwanted competition, dealers or wholesalers are disinclined to give information on markets and sources to anyone, but they are especially reluctant to talk to fishermen. No dealer wants to admit to lowering prices. Dealers have several ways of obscuring the way prices are changed and their own role in the process. They talk about price movements as if magical forces, rather than human decisions, were responsible: 'the price is moving up.' "*

For many fishermen the dealer's authority was inescapable because—especially in the 1940s and 1950s—the dealer was virtually their banker. Some were indebted to dealers for staking them large sums to help buy boats and gear. Others habitually bought their fuel, gear, and bait from a dealer, at cost or a small markup. A steady supply of bait is most important to the fishermen, and dealers sometimes have not hesitated to use their control over it to bring mavericks into line. But dealers also gave to fishermen who "fished for me" the assurance that they would buy their catch any and every day (at a price, to be sure, set by the dealer). Acheson describes this exchange as entirely rational on the fishermen's part, since they surrender a right to bargain, one that is weak or nonexistant anyway, for things of immediate practical worth.

* James Acheson, *The Lobster Gangs of Maine* (Hanover, N.H., 1988), p. 126.

Thus many lobstermen and dealers historically developed a special relationship. In 1885 one observer described the visit of lobster smacks to Deer Island: "The skipper [of each vessel] endeavors to attach to him his special gang, or *clientele,* and to make it as large as possible. To insure that they shall fish for him and no other, he uses all the arts of the commercial traveler. He makes a slightly more favorable price here, relies upon an exhibition of jolly good-fellowship there, and appeals to long-established usage and other motives elsewhere. He must be able, too, to fit a man out on credit, now and then, with the necessary gear for the campaign. By every means in his power he assures him that he will do better with no other living skipper, and begs him not to forget it."

One of Portland's wholesale lobster dealers of the 1950s echoed this account: "I'd always give the fishermen [who sold regularly to me] a little tickle here and there or somethin' . . . paying a little more at times for loyalty." A retired fisherman told of a meeting of disgruntled draggermen and lobstermen in Portland, who had gathered to talk about cooperating to get better prices. (The dealers' special relationships with "their" men usually has meant that they are kept well informed of any movements among fishermen inimical to their interests.) Into the meeting suddenly burst a well-known wholesaler, George Lewis, with a bottle of whiskey in each hand. Plunging into the group, he handed out the bottles, called for glasses, and ended the meeting by proclaiming, "Dinner's on me at Vallee's [a local steak-and-fish house]." "He bought us off with a couple of hundred dollars," said the fisherman, "*and it was our money.*"

While distrust of dealers had always tinged the relationship, that distrust grew more intense after 1950 as the retail value of the product rose but the boat price seemed to lag behind. Veterans came home from the war, too, with new perspectives and new sources of financing, so fishermen slowly loosed the bonds tying them to dealers. At the same time, they became convinced that the larger dealers constituted a standing conspiracy to cheat them.

Obviously, some exaggeration entered into lobstermen's attitudes about price. To some extent the "law of supply and demand," as dealers liked to say, did operate autonomously. Yet even Acheson, who believes that price is determined initially by "impersonal market forces," admitted that dealers did hoard information and did talk to one another constantly. "The Portland and Boston dealers, as one man expressed it [to Acheson], 'all have their heads together.' "

Given the reputed independence of the breed, lobstermen's "cooperatives" sounds like an oxymoron. But amid the swelling tide of suspicion concerning dealers' practices, cooperatives began to take hold in the late 1940s. Cooperatives, because they try to pay their members top prices, did succeed, at least in the areas where they existed, in providing a yardstick against which to compare dealers' prices.

Ironically, the dealers' secrecy which the MLA and cooperatives tried to transcend has been paralleled by just as powerful a habit of secretiveness among fishermen when dealing with one another. Lobster fishermen compete intensely, believing that they are engaged in a zero-sum game: they think there are a finite number of lobsters of legal size in a given area. Competition among "highliners"—fishermen with established reputations for catching many lobsters—is especially fierce, as is their reluctance to talk about catch, technique, productive grounds and, often, the price being paid to *them.* Seldom do fishermen boast of having a good year or making money, though they often let the purchase of a new truck or some other big-ticket item speak for itself.

A group so highly competitive and secretive presented formidable obstacles to organization. Even some of the ways in which lobstermen were knit together made cooperation beyond the local level difficult. Acheson, who has written eloquently of the fishermen's compulsive competitiveness, at the same time has debunked the Lone Ranger image of romantic individualism, arguing that contrary to appearances, lobster fishermen are "caught up in a thick and complex web of social relationships." He says that the basic social units of lobstering are "harbor gangs" into which individuals must be accepted before they can pursue their livelihood successfully. Men fish in territory "owned" and defended by particular harbor gangs. The segmented coastline of peninsulas and islands creates the geographic base for the harbor gangs, and a sense of great distance or hostility may be felt toward neighboring villages that are really not very far away. Fishermen in rival gangs from the next landfall down the coast will be thought of as "strange," or "cunners" or "shit-kickin' farmers." In the 1950s Chebeague Island men in Casco Bay would almost spit out a uniquely pejorative term for fishermen from a rival harbor: "dung eyes."

Fishermen in Casco Bay say that the harbor-gang culture is now, as with so many traditions of lobstering, far more a Down East thing. In the 1950s, however, these networks retained vitality in Casco Bay and the midcoast, meaning that both individualism and the less obvious bonds of lobstermen inhibited cooperation from east to west.

Yet the MLA grew rapidly after 1955, in part because the fishery faced new threats as well as increased pressure from old ones. An offshore lobster fishery had begun recently as deep-water vessels trawling for groundfish at the edge of the continental shelf netted lobsters, many of which were throwbacks in their huge size to colonial days. In 1950, 300,000 pounds of mostly jumbos were taken; by 1960, 1.2 million pounds. Maine lobstermen believe, along with marine biologists, that big lobsters are the principal source of stock replenishing, and that the big offshore breeders produce millions of fry which move back inshore to feed. Draggers were not only rivals, but posed a major threat to the resource.

In the 1950s, too, the debate over the impact of Canadian imports heated up. This debate had gone on since the 1920s, when the Canadian catch entered the market in a big way. Most dealers have maintained that Canadian lobsters do not depress the U.S. price, especially since the Canadian fishing season runs from December to Memorial Day. Many of these are "pounded" (i.e., put in holding pens called pounds), but dealers say that most are out of the pounds by the Fourth of July. Maine fishermen believe the contrary—that whenever else they might be sold, Canadian lobsters are also released on the U.S. market at the peak New England fishing season from July on. The dealers' most telling argument, however, is that Maine and New England production overall is not enough to supply the U.S. market (which is why Canadian lobsters come in duty-free).

This is one of those debates that seems destined to be endless, but a bit of history provided by Martin and Lipfert in *Lobstering and the Maine Coast* is instructive. In 1919 the Canadian canning industry was fading, and big U.S. fish companies were poised to exploit a cheap source of lobsters. In that year Maine's average price per pound was

24.7 cents, and the average in New Brunswick, Prince Edward Island, and Nova Scotia ranged from 7.3 to 10.8 cents. Twenty years later the average in the Maritimes was 9.5, but the Maine price had fallen to 15.6 cents. "Eastern Maine pounds," say Martin and Lipfert with understated humor, "were being used as 'rest stops' for the naturalization of Canadian critters on their way to U.S. markets." Wholesalers here had found a reliable and cheap supply of lobsters, and tended to exploit it in the late summer and fall. Most galling of all to Maine fishermen is the fact that most Canadian lobsters are marketed to tourists and shoppers as "Maine lobsters."

In the fifties, too, the "rock lobster" reared what was to Maine fishermen its ugly tail. Imports of crawfish from South Africa in particular but also from Australia and Central America began to move into U.S. markets, again duty-free. Lobstermen scorned this product as a mushy fraud, but it contributed to the economic pinch.

The postwar economic growth of the 1950s established the United States as the world's preeminent consumer society. In Maine, as elsewhere, the fruits of affluence became visible as television aerials sprouted along the coast and as fishermen's appetite for material goods similarly expanded. These pressures made cooperation in the MLA compellingly attractive for fishermen. The association grew spectacularly from 1954 to 1958, though the numbers involved have always been subject to debate. Some skeptics have doubted Dyer's claim of 2,500 members in 1957, but no one doubts that MLA sympathizers and fellow travelers constituted by 1957–58 a majority of the full-time lobster fishermen. What pulled men into the MLA, and what brought non–dues payers into temporary alliance, was Les Dyer's honing in on the matter of a minimum price. And that launched Dyer and the MLA onto a collision course with the dealers and eventually with the U.S. government.

2 "A TIE-UP, NOT A STRIKE!"

n 1956 the reigning boss of the Portland waterfront was an unprepossessing, soft-spoken man in his forties, of average height, roundish, with receding light-brown hair turning silver and brown eyes. Most working days he wore a white shirt open at the collar to his office on Central Wharf, where his employees called him "Jack." But his eyes threw off a hard glint.

John E. Willard Jr., a Yale University graduate, had inherited control of the Willard-Daggett seafood company from his father. His grandfather had operated a vessel in the coastal trade between Maine and Georgia, coming ashore about 1908 to devote himself entirely to a wholesale fish business that originated with William Daggett as a partner in 1880. The Willards, however, were the primary owners, and John's father and most of his six siblings also worked in the family business, which by 1928 was "the most complete fish-handling plant" in Maine, with a fleet of twelve fishing vessels, three lobster pounds, a smokehouse, cold-storage plant, and—according to a puff piece in the local newspaper—"excellent" salt curing facilities. In the mid-1930s,

Willard-Daggett sent weekly shipments of lobsters, scallops, and other delicacies to Franklin Roosevelt's White House. By the 1950s, when Jack took over control from his father, lobster sales were dominating the company's business, and Willard-Daggett was dominating the supply of lobsters to Portland-area restaurants and grocery stores.

Born in 1909, Jack was in the prime of manhood when he succeeded his father as the leading figure in Portland's fish commerce. At twenty-one he graduated from college and went directly into the business. In 1940, when the company underwent one of several reorganizations during its history and John A. Tonneson was brought in as president and manager, Jack became his assistant while John Sr. became treasurer, still retaining great influence. (The Tonnesons would be among those who bought out the Willard interest in the 1970s.) Soon Jack would be given the title of vice-president, but it was not until 1952 that he took charge of the company and stepped into his father's shoes as the man with the most influence over the lobster boat-price from Casco Bay to the Penobscot.

Some eight to ten dealers bought lobsters from fishermen and draggers on the Portland and South Portland docks, but Jack Willard, said Bernard Johnson, was "king." A wholesaler who worked for Willard during that period put it pungently: "He run the whole f——n' waterfront." Every morning Jack would be at his phone, calling the other dealers and telling them what the price would be that day. "Willard's old man used to quote the price and set things and Jack just came into his office and took over," recalled a former dealer. Rival dealers might choose, of course, to defy him, but it was well known that if you crossed a Willard, they would exact a revenge that would cost you. Jack's older brother Phil, after practicing law in Boston for three years, moved his practice to Portland and participated in the family business from 1933 on. He said that Jack "fought like hell" with other dealers. "I remember that he and my father, if they could make a competitor lose money, that was better than making money."

So Jack Willard maneuvered first to dominate his dealer-competitors in Casco Bay and vicinity. He could be affable and trade jokes with other dealers or fishermen as easily as he could move in the elite circles of Portland's commercial society, though playing golf with local lawyers or executives was more to his liking than, say, dining at the stodgy Cumberland Club up a few blocks from the wharves.

"His wharf was his world," and within that sphere information was power, information was money, and he sought both to hoard and to control its flow. He loved the game, and at its first level the players were his local competitors; then came the more powerful and less tractable dealers of, say, Boston and Rockland.

Among the resources he employed to dominate other dealers were lobster pounds: essentially these were fenced-off coves or other natural pens where the summer and fall catch of soft-shell lobsters could be stored in an almost natural habitat through the winter while their shells hardened. The survivors could be sold later at far higher prices. Willard would sometimes pay "ungodly high prices" for lobsters during the winter and early spring, because that would drive up the price of his pounded lobsters. Jack ran pounds "all over the place," from nearby Cliff Island to Friendship, Grand Manan, and offshore Matinicus Island.

"His" lobster fishermen were simply part of the arsenal he used in the competition to beat his rivals. The fishermen, pretense aside, were hardly equals, and control of them came to Jack Willard as a habitual and taken-for-granted exercise of power. Controlling lobstercatchers required attention, of course, but in dealing with these fishermen Willard enjoyed enormous leverage.

As other dealers had for generations, Willard bought lobsters mostly from a regular retinue of catchers. At least 40 percent of the Portland-area fishermen sold to Jack Willard. Some were tied to Willard by loyalty and good treatment, some he had loaned money, and some had been staked early in their careers by his father. For many, "he had 'em, money wise. They didn't like the idea, but he had 'em." A former dealer who operated at a nearby dock described the quiet effectiveness with which Willard exercised his power. "All of a sudden, I'd look out the window, or my foreman would say, 'hey we got a new boat comin' in,' and I'd go out and see this boat and talk to the fisherman. And then my foreman would come to me and say, '. . . telephone call.' And I'd go in and hear: 'This is Jack next door. I would really appreciate your not buying from the boat. He owes me a lot of money.' And I would say, 'you got it, Jack.' I'd just go out, and, hey, I might not tell the guy why. I'd say I'm crowded, I haven't got room, I can't buy anything from you."

Dealers and fishermen always knew where Jack Willard stood, and he was known for his honesty. Some dealers had reputations for playing tricks with their scales, but not Willard. No fisherman doubted Willard's weighings of the catch. But none doubted that Willard called the tune and that he could be "just plain cruel at times," offering rock-bottom prices for fish or lobsters. Thus many fishermen harbored a concealed but deep resentment of Jack Willard.

Willard-Daggett's reaction to the Maine Lobstermen's Association might have been foreshadowed by the aggressive history of the company and by its fight with the Seafood Workers' Union, an American Federation of Labor affiliate, back in 1939–40. Thirty-one-year-old Jack had been the company spokesman, dealing with the press and the union representatives. The union had forced seven Portland wholesalers into negotiations when its Boston locals stopped delivery of fish to and from Boston. The local Truckman's Union was cooperating with the Seafood Workers and would cross no picket lines. Willard, however, would not meet with the Boston organizer, John Lind, to discuss union demands affecting the wages and hours of some forty fish handlers and cutters until Lind showed him that his union represented a majority of Willard-Daggett employees. Of course, Willard wanted to know *who* among his workers was bringing in the union. The dealers—though not Willard—agreed to attend a conference, but when Lind refused to produce the list of workers he represented, the dealers walked out. The union called a strike the next day, but Willard-Daggett men worked. The Willards' resistance would delay settlement for months.

The year 1956 began with a Portland lobster dealer other than Willard attracting attention all along the coast because of a provocative speech to a Lions Club in South Portland. Addressing in part the same issue of chief concern to the Maine Lobstermen's Association—namely, low boat prices during shedder season—William V. Benson raised a storm on both sides of the docks by decrying the quality of shedder lobsters and by proposing a closed season from July to November in order to give the new-shell lobsters a chance to harden, fill out with

meat, and become less perishable. For the mid-twentieth-century lobster industry, this was rank heresy. Both the MLA and the dealers,
joined by Fisheries Commissioner Stanley Tupper, criticized Benson
for his "damaging outburst," his "disservice" to the fishery, and above
all his "sullying the reputation of the Maine lobster." Les Dyer pointed
out that Benson's suggestion would close the fishery during the time
when demand was highest and when three-fourths of the lobstermen
made most of their income. While conceding that the shedder did
contain less meat than hard-shell lobsters, it was, said Dyer, far more
delicious. Benson further riled Dyer and the MLA by endorsing offshore dragging of lobsters.

Benson was impolitic to stress the negatives of shedders, yet parts
of what he said have appealed to thoughtful fishermen and dealers
over the years. For example, Benson would gladly have bid good-bye to
the part-time, summer fishermen. He proposed staggering the fishing
season as was done in Canada and closing the coast in stages, beginning in the southwest (where the shedders appear first). Professional
fishermen, he said, "would bring in just as many lobsters in the long
run and they would be of better quality."

The influential Rockland dealer Harold Look also deplored the bad
publicity that Benson had visited upon the Maine lobster. Yet Look was
attracted by the idea of a staggered season, even though he thought it
needed to last only two or three weeks in each sector. He pointed to the
island of Monhegan, where the fishing season began in January and
whose fishermen were now being paid 60 cents a pound for fewer but
much heavier lobsters. Look also put his finger on an important point
that Dyer and Tupper, for the moment at least, had ignored: "We do
have problems such as almost three-quarters of our yearly catch produced in a few months following the shedding season, causing a temporary over-supply and too cheap a price."

"Too cheap a price." While this fact seemed lost in the debate of
winter, in the June 1956 convention of the MLA at Rockland it clearly
sat foremost in the fishermen's minds. In September 1955, following in
the well-worn path of post–Labor Day price cuts and in the wake of
hurricanes that sent tourists scurrying prematurely out of Maine, the
late-season boat price had plummeted to 25 cents a pound, and many
MLA fishermen were ready for a fight. First, however, the men and

their wives listened to speeches from Governor Edmund Muskie and Commissioner Tupper, then were entertained by vaudeville acts, a late floor show, and marine supply companies' exhibits. Getting down to business, the association went on record as favoring a half-cent per pound industry tax to promote and advertise lobsters, a uniform lobster-gauge for the eastern seaboard, and a ban on imports of Canadian lobster meat taken from shellfish under the Maine minimum. But the main item on the agenda was summed up in the headline of the July *Maine Coast Fisherman:* "Maine Lobstermen's Association Votes Minimum Price of 35¢ for Shedders, 50¢ for Old Shells."

Throughout July and August 1956 the price held, and various news reports credited the MLA with stabilizing the market. But in September, soon after Labor Day, Jack Willard put out the word that the price was going to be 30 cents. Immediately two huge Massachusetts lobster companies with pounds throughout Maine, James Hook and Consolidated, gave notice that they too would pay only 30 cents. Willard's representative said that dealers could not pay over 30 cents because out-of-state demand had fallen sharply with summer's end, and many dealers were saddled with lobsters for which they had paid 40 to 45 cents.

Willard's bombshell had fallen in Portland late on a Monday, September 10. What happened next could not have taken place before World War II, when most fishermen were not equipped with short-wave radios. The MLA sprang into action over telephones and ship radios, asking members and their harbormates to stay in and not fish. Some were hailed from boats. Not everyone came in, of course, or stayed in, but the message spread with astonishing rapidity.

The tie-up, as it was called, began in Portland after a meeting of fishermen on the wharves, and by Tuesday night an estimated three to four hundred Casco Bay fishing boats lay fast by their moorings, while some twenty thousand Bay traps were "laid over." In the Rockland area, Leslie Dyer had gone on the radio to plead with association members to back the Casco men and stop fishing until a "living wage" was offered. Dyer told newspaper reporters that dealers outside Portland were still paying 35 cents, and he denied the dealer rationale of a glut of lobsters: "The market hasn't dropped [enough] to warrant a 30 cent lobster." Fishermen, he emphasized, must be paid at least 35 cents to show a profit. "Last June," he added, "lobstermen agreed on 35 cents a pound as a minimum."

The Casco men soon heard the encouraging news that Harpswell and Bailey Island fishermen, just to the east, had joined the tie-up, even though they were still getting paid 35 cents. By Thursday the tie-up had spread through Penobscot Bay and beyond. Dyer and other MLA officers were holding meetings with fishermen at island and coastal harbors, and the MLA was claiming that some four thousand to forty-five hundred lobstermen had stopped fishing. However reliable these figures may have been, the Rockland *Courier-Gazette* accurately noted that the events of the week of September 10 "never had been seen before along the shores of Maine."

Dealer reaction varied along the coast, since some had never paid below 35 cents. Even in Portland at least one dealer expressed sympathy for the fishermen and termed the 35 cent minimum "justified." Les Dyer claimed that most dealers *outside* Portland agreed with the MLA's price floor. The dealers who fought the tie-up, continuing to encourage men to fish, kept pointing to the abnormally high prices that they had been paying in August, up to 40–45 cents. Now, however, Bill Benson would pay no more than 30 cents, and Jack Willard, who had announced the price in Portland, insisted that the decline of out-of-state demand dictated a price cut. Willard scoffed at the MLA, claiming that the tie-up did not hurt dealers since it gave them a chance to clear out excess inventory from their holding tanks. At the same time, though, Willard wanted men to keep fishing for him at the 30 cent price.

Jack Willard would hardly reveal any of his real market strategies to the newspapers. Willard and other dealers were not in the habit of publicizing their calculations, engaged as they were in a highly competitive business obsessively dependent on secrecy and manipulation of the market. It is certain that Willard and other dealers detested the idea of fishermen bargaining with them as equals. Also they believed the tie-up was bad for business: by publicizing low boat prices the controversy created the wrong impression among consumers, who then went to markets or restaurants looking for bargain-basement lobster prices. Disappointed shoppers then turned to other seafoods, further depressing demand.

Next to the all-important matter of price, the issue of dealer control lay at the heart of the dispute. With the MLA's leadership, fishermen were asserting a new independence of dealers. Jack Willard, for one, was not pleased with that development.

Spokesmen for the MLA repeatedly claimed that they believed a new understanding with dealers had been reached—which the abrupt, preemptory price cut had violated. MLA officials said that dealers had assured them that in the event of a glut, instead of dropping the price "dealers would ask the lobstermen to hold up for a period and enable dealers to relieve the over-supply." As negotiations brought the tie-up to an end, the fishermen would again assert that this agreement had been reached with "the dealers" (including, by implication, Jack Willard).

On Saturday, finally, MLA representative Rodney Cushing went to the Willard-Daggett office to meet with Jack Willard. Cushing was a thirty-six-year-old lobster fisherman from Cliff Island, a small scenic wonder at the eastern edge of Casco Bay. Cushing had been born on Cliff, the son and grandson of fishermen. He had begun lobstering after high school with his father, then went on his own in a large outboard skiff. After naval service in World War II, Cushing had reentered lobstering and became active in the MLA at its founding.

Tall and handsome, with a sharply chiseled face featuring prominent eyebrows and ice-blue eyes, Cushing spoke in a clear, well-modulated voice and, unlike many fishermen, clearly enjoyed words and speaking. Talking with Cushing in his seventies, it is easy to see why the lobstermen would send him as a delegate to deal with Willard. Tactful and circumspect, Cushing possessed the skills of a politician and a diplomat. He would be smoothly deferential and not offend Willard, yet he could be counted on to convey firmly the position of the fishermen.

The week-long tie-up produced a victory for the lobstermen. They would resume hauling on Monday, the 17th of September, at 35 cents. And, again, Cushing came out of the meeting saying that the dealers had assured the MLA it would be given notice before any drop in price below 35 cents. The October 1956 *Maine Coast Fisherman* again said it all: "M.L.A. Wins Lobster Battle, Minimum Price Back to 35 Cents." Fishermen went back to work in a mood of celebration, their radios crackling with jokes about all the lobsters they could expect to find in their set-over traps and with self-congratulations on their rare show of unity.

The stage was now set for a repeat the following year of an eerily similar pattern of events, but this time the outcome would be far different. The tie-up's success had produced some angry dealers. Willard kept his thoughts to himself, but the outspoken Bill Benson protested that fishermen had used coercion to enforce the tie-up. Benson claimed that "our [his] fishermen" continued to fish at 30 cents, but that they were threatened by strikers and at least one loyalist had suffered damage to his traps. Benson complained also that the local warden lacked boats to protect those men who wanted to fish (the warden replied that no dealer or fisherman had requested protection). Tie-up coercion, however, would soon become an extremely important issue.

The controversy to come would dwarf that of 1956 and would be resolved ultimately in a federal courtroom. Its underlying cause may be understood at a glance. In 1956 Maine lobstermen landed just under 20.6 million pounds, which brought in $9,119,807; in 1957 the catch rose to just over 24.4 million pounds, but for a return of only $8,954,234. The average price in 1956 was 44 cents; in 1957, 37 cents.

That summer the coast warmed up quickly and the shedders came early. Canadian lobsters, usually off the market in quantity by June, were still coming in July. And to make matters worse, Railway Express went on strike, cutting off wholesalers' access to Midwestern and Southern markets.

The spring had begun, however, on a note of cooperation between dealers and the MLA. Even though they delivered opposing testimony to the Maine legislature about new legislation that would increase the minimum length of Maine lobsters from three and one-eighth inches to three and three-sixteenth inches (dealers favoring, MLA opposing), the disagreement was amicable, and then the MLA joined dealers in supporting an increase to a maximum length of five and three-sixteenth inches. In its annual June convention the MLA once again voted to stand by the 35 cent minimum price in the months ahead. A test of their resolve lay just days away.

Out of the blue on Tuesday, July 16, 1957, Portland dealers cut the price on soft-shell lobsters to 30 cents (old shells held at 50 cents).

On Wednesday most Casco Bay lobstermen either did not leave their moorings or were persuaded to come in by supporters of a tie-up. Over a hundred tight-jawed fishermen had gathered at the Portland docks and held a meeting on the roof of the Harris Company ship chandlery; they refused to fish. Leslie Dyer rushed to Portland to talk to the fishermen and circulated a letter to MLA delegates calling for a meeting in Rockland on Friday to "take appropriate action on the 30¢ price now being imposed on us."

The delegates, with many other fishermen and interested parties in attendance, met at the GAR Hall in Rockland and voted unanimously to support the Portland tie-up. Angry delegates made sarcastic remarks about Portland dealers and, recognizing that some fishermen in Casco Bay refused to tie up and that other mavericks would do the same down the coast, suggested that forms of persuasion other than words might get "hard-shelled" nonmembers in line. While many fishermen had joined the tie-up by week's end, the fact was that west of Casco Bay in the tourist-populated areas near the New Hampshire border, most fishermen were still hauling traps and dealers were doing a brisk business. Les Dyer in his calm, genial manner spiked the talk of violence when questioned by reporters: "It's all pure rumor. No violence is expected and we have warned our members against any such foolishness."

Though some dealers west and east of Portland were paying 35 cents and more, Willard, Benson, and their associates stubbornly refused to pay more than 30 cents (or 32 at their wharves). Dyer tried to get their attention by claiming that the MLA was negotiating with "powerful" out-of-state seafood interests to bypass local dealers. But several Portland dealers countered by announcing that they intended to close both Sunday and Monday until fishermen would be willing to fish for the "correct price."

The week of Monday, July 22, began with more meetings of fishermen in Portland and other harbors in and around Casco Bay. Their frustration mounted as the dealers refused negotiation offers carried to them by the MLA's Rodney Cushing. Scarborough fishermen had never stopped hauling, and on Tuesday night a few Saco Bay lobstermen voted to fish, while Bailey Island, Orr's Island, and Harpswell men had never been firmly committed to the tie-up. By now, threats and recriminations were rife in Casco Bay, and on Wednesday three lobster boats were berthed overnight at the Coast Guard base in South Portland because their owners feared they might be damaged if left at their usual moorings. The owners were said to be getting "sweetheart" or "under the table" arrangements with dealers.

By midweek the MLA decided to shift tactics, a move that led quickly to the defeat of the tie-up and an outpouring of outrage from MLA militants in Casco Bay. Dyer announced that all fishermen should go out again but sell only to those dealers who were paying at least 35 cents per pound. He had received many phone calls, he said, telling him that few dealers outside Casco Bay were paying less than 35 cents, and those businesses should not be punished. A Tuesday-afternoon phone polling of the executive board had led to the decision. This essentially ended the tie-up outside Casco Bay, but in Portland MLA members were thunderstruck. On Thursday morning Leslie Dyer, Alan Grossman, and other MLA officers met with Casco fishermen, again assembled in the open sunshine atop the Harris Company roof, and faced a firestorm of protest.

Lobster fishermen's meetings are not governed by *Robert's Rules of Order,* but fishermen normally will listen quietly once someone has their attention, and they will listen especially to someone they respect, such as "highliners" or harbor-gang leaders. The July 25 meeting began quietly enough, with both Leslie Dyer and Alan Grossman reminding the men that membership in the MLA was voluntary, that the association was not a union, and that it could not tell its own members, let alone nonmembers, what to do. Individuals were at liberty to sell their lobsters for 10 cents or to give them away if they chose. "You are the sole proprietor of your business. That's the American way of life. We don't dictate to you." Grossman and Dyer also tried to put the best face possible on the MLA's signaling its members to sell to dealers who would pay 35 cents. But this did not dampen the fury of the Casco Bay men.

Bad enough that local "scabs" could now justify their self-interested actions, but betrayal by their own association was even worse. What the protesters resented most was that the MLA, by renewing a strong supply of catch to the east and west of Casco Bay, made it easy for Portland's dealers to ignore them and to buy "on both sides of us."

As it was, even before the MLA's shift, Portland dealers were known to be buying up and down the coast and were paying 35 cents to nonlocal fishermen. This knowledge reinforced the belief which had grown during the week among MLA fishermen and officials that the major purpose of the price cut had been to whip Casco Bay fishermen back into line. Most men on the rooftop agreed with Dyer that "the whole purpose of the local dealers is to break the lobstermen in Casco Bay and then break those along the remainder of the coast." The issues were price and power. The heart of the conflict was the MLA's presumption to bargain with dealers.

Dyer addressed the men's anger: "I know you fellows are not happy about this. I haven't had a night's sleep since the decision. It wasn't pleasant." Some still shouted their disapproval, while others yelled support of Dyer, or got up to defend him as still their friend and ally, however mistaken. The discussion turned uglier when Elroy Johnson of Bailey Island rose to dissent from Dyer and the majority.

The Bailey Island men fished mostly from Mackerel Cove, a harbor whose natural beauty was such that, if the gods had decided to be fishermen, they would have nestled their boats there. Few Bailey Island men had joined the tie-up, and not for long in any case. Johnson, a well-known highliner, criticized the MLA for acting like a union and for impulsively calling a tie-up. He disputed Dyer's claim that fishermen could not make a profit selling at 30 cents—he could, he said. Many men began to shout before he finished, hooting at his claims of profit at 30 cents, sarcastically suggesting he hire them to work with him. Dyer calmed things down and responded good-naturedly that "Elroy has got his figures twisted," emphatically asserting: "We don't want a union." But if lobstermen accepted less than 35 cents now, he stressed, "we would be selling a 25 cent lobster on Labor Day." Next time, said Dyer, every one will "go out" and stay out until there is one price for all.

An hour and a half of debate resolved nothing, and the anger had not subsided. At noon Dyer announced that Philip F. Chapman Jr., a local attorney and former state senator, had arranged for a meeting with the dealer William Benson. Chapman, Dyer, Grossman, and Cushing went off to meet with Benson, who conferred with other dealers by phone during the afternoon. By 5 P.M. Dyer grimly reported back to the fishermen: "Absolutely nothing going." The dealers "felt they had us over a barrel and would keep us there." Sarcastic joking from the Casco fishermen greeted Dyer's next piece of bad news. He had learned during the afternoon that central Maine dealers who had been paying 35 cents had dropped to 30. Dyer conceded that they were defeated for now, but exhorted the men to stand firm: "They say they will bust you as an association; let's show them that we won't [quit]. . . . We are down but not out. The last battle is the best one to win." With that, Dyer called for an MLA meeting in Rockland on Monday the 29th.

Any systematic tie-up was over for now: some Casco Bay men had not fished from July 17 to 25, and some diehards would stay in through the weekend. By Monday most Bay fishermen were "hauling like mad," but since the price drop had arrived at the central coast, boats there were now coming in and sentiment was building for another stoppage. By the end of the day, the MLA indeed called for all six thousand or so lobstermen to tie up until they won a 35 cent minimum for the entire coast.

The Rockland-Penobscot-area fishermen, now getting 30 cents, cooperated with the MLA during the first part of the week. Now the question was, would Casco Bay men, thinking themselves let down by their midcoast neighbors the week before, once again join a tie-up, which some reporters, dealers, and fishermen were calling a "strike." MLA officials, however, began at this point to insist carefully that their membership not refer to the tie-up as a strike. This became an MLA mantra the length of the coast: "A tie-up, not a strike!"

That slogan was Les Dyer's message to a hundred or so Portland lobstermen meeting at 4 P.M. on Wednesday, July 31, on the Harris Company roof, now baking at the end of a hot day. Some of the men, already not working, had been breaking the tedium by drinking beer or nips of stronger stuff, which only added to making the meeting memorably "hot and heavy." Now a much more vocal minority opposed the tie-up, and MLA militants believed that Jack Willard had prompted some fishermen to speak out against another tie-up. Some were still angry at Dyer for signaling midcoast men to sell selectively while Casco Bay had not been fishing. Others immediately rallied to his defense: "He's entitled to make one mistake. Even President Eisenhower has made a lot." Dyer, urging them to tie up again, claimed that four thousand fishermen had stopped or were about to stop hauling. He said that the fishermen east of Casco Bay now had their eyes opened by getting paid 30 cents themselves: "They needed a shock to see what you fellows were up against."

The majority agreed with Dyer, but Bernard Johnson of Bailey Island, an even-tempered moderate, rose to remind the group that men there and on Harpswell were still fishing, and he balked at going along with the MLA. This prompted a good deal of muttering, and Johnson heard some militants (who he believed had been drinking) whispering in the background about throwing him off the roof.

One wholly unpersuaded dissenter was the highliner Evans Doughty of Two Lights, Cape Elizabeth, a lean, fiftyish, sunburned fisherman wearing large eyeglasses and the fisherman's typical visored cap. Doughty had stayed out for a time earlier, but fully intended to fish now no matter what the meeting decided. Squinting into the sun, he angrily defended his constitutional right to fish if he wanted and, anticipating threats, furiously warned that if his boat or gear were damaged he would "go through the association" and "there wouldn't be a buoy left in the whole ocean."

Dyer replied with his familiar line that without the MLA, dealers would now probably be paying as little as 25 cents, and he added there was something drastically wrong with the boat price since soft- and hard-shell lobsters were retailing now for 69 and 89 cents a pound. He repeated his conviction, echoed by others, that Portland dealers were pushing the price down not only to take unfair advantage of them, but especially to break the MLA as a force in price negotiations. Dyer reached for a consensus by playing his hole card: the MLA would appeal to Governor Edmund Muskie to settle the dispute, and Dyer had learned that Muskie was willing to try to broker a settlement. Claiming that public opinion favored the fishermen, Dyer said: "You have shown that you have the guts to stay out. Governor Muskie will see to it that you boys get justice." But when the meeting finally voted, twenty-five men held out against a tie-up while sixty-nine voted for it. Some men did not vote, and a few had already left. Casco Bay would tie up again, but it was already clear that the action would not be unanimous.

When Bernard Johnson returned to Bailey Island to report the MLA decision, he ran into a buzz saw of contention. Most of the fishermen there tied up for three or four days, at most, during both the July and the August tie-up. Johnson and others were "lugging our lobsters all the way 'round to Small Point," where a dealer was still paying 35 cents. As Johnson approached one fisherman, the man stepped onto the dock brandishing a pitchfork and swore no one would make him stay in.

On Chebeague Island, the largest in Casco Bay, with some thirty fishermen, the MLA delegate Alger Burgess was at home one morning, several days after the meeting at the Harris Company, when "a gang of the boys" appeared to say that they needed to go back out hauling. Alger pleaded with them to stay in. "Alger," they said, "we got bills to pay and we need to put food on the table." Alger and his wife, Shirley, happened to have a large turkey in the refrigerator, so she put it in the oven and invited the men to come back with their wives for dinner. Yet while Chebeague was more unified than Bailey Island (some of the men who fished out of Mackerel Cove lived in Brunswick or even farther away), it too had mavericks. One unpopular man was using a feud with another lobsterman to justify going out to fish.

Down East the tie-up experienced similar problems. In the Prospect Harbor, Gouldsboro, and Corea area, many fishermen tied up in August, but one or two harbor-gang leaders resisted. The MLA delegate Elmer Alley told Les Dyer that one of the ringleaders of opposition at Corea even "draws a good government pension" and was hardly strapped for cash.

One Portland dealer, Roland Hurtubise, questioned MLA claims to have effectively tied up the whole coast. "I've got men fishing for me right now—and I can prove it—in Casco Bay and Harpswell. Each of these lobstermen," he claimed, "will bring me between 500 and 1,000 pounds of lobsters per day. At 30 cents a pound, that's between $150 and $300 for a day's work. Is there anything wrong with that?"

On Saturday, August 3, a letter from Governor Muskie to Les Dyer appeared in the Rockland *Courier-Gazette,* proposing that a fact-finding committee be formed of fishermen and dealers, and that the two sides should meet together to resolve the dispute. Action on the state's part, however, would be inappropriate. Dyer welcomed the letter, but it was not clear just what would come of it. Muskie had sent the letter also to the Rockland dealer Harold Look, and had asked Look to chair a meeting of dealers and to induce them to negotiate. Look, a square-jawed, gray-haired patriarch whose steel-rimmed eyeglasses accented his stern visage and strong opinions, agreed with Dyer and the MLA on several matters, but he was also a forceful proponent of the dealers' viewpoint.

On Monday, August 5, Look succeeded in getting Jack Willard, Arthur Colwell of Deer Isle, and other dealers to come to Rockland. He hoped to have a committee meet with dealers along all three sections of the coast, but it soon became clear that Look's colleagues preferred not to budge and not to pay 35 cents. They insisted that they could not move shedders at that price, nor make a profit. Meeting in the morning and afternoon, the dealers disclosed nothing at the end of the day. Apparently no further meetings would take place. The dealers had taken a vote and were sending a letter to Muskie, but, in keeping with their habitual secrecy, Look was not at liberty to disclose the nature of either. The only reasonable inference to be drawn from these Vaticanlike puffs of smoke was that the dealers were stonewalling the fishermen and counting on their disunity. One even suggested that no disagreement existed between dealers and fishermen, and that any dispute was among the fishermen themselves. The next day, Dyer called for an emergency meeting of the MLA in Rockland, on Wednesday, August 7.

The Rockland Community Building resembled hundreds across small-town America: a large, antiseptic auditorium of concrete, wood, and steel with movable glass basketball backboards suspended from the ceiling at each end. Several hundred fishermen along with dozens of interested parties filled the building that Wednesday. Newspaper photos of the audience reveal a weatherworn crowd of rugged men matter-of-factly gazing at the stage and podium. Sober and determined, they wanted a vote on whether to continue to tie up. Before voting, though, the men heard from a variety of speakers, from the stage and the floor.

Leslie Dyer introduced Harold Look, whose attendance the governor had recommended. Dyer described Look as an old friend and a fair man, but one with whom he did not see eye to eye. "We are friends . . . but as far apart as the poles." Look was listened to respectfully as he advocated a rotary closed season, a ban on Sunday fishing (enthusiastically received), and a uniform lobster-gauge that would include the

Canadians. But when Look urged the men to obey the law of supply and demand and return to fishing, they began to shout their disagreement. Then they pressed him with pointed questions about price, but Look would not answer; Dyer stepped in and reminded the men that Look was there at the governor's request and, in any case, deserved to be treated with courtesy.

Others spoke, including Alan Grossman and a big, red-faced fellow from Deer Isle who honestly and simply said he did not want to tie up, bringing down a chorus of boos. Alger Burgess of Chebeague came forward to say that "if we go back to fishing at 30 cents then we're just a bunch of idiots"—and was wildly cheered. Before the ballot, Les Dyer endorsed a tie-up and spoke in his engaging, preacherly manner about the need to "convert the heathen." A number of unbelievers, however, infested the hall, and the vote, after three hours of discussion, many departures, and some abstaining, registered 250 in favor of persisting and 94 for fishing.

Even as five-sevenths of those voting in Rockland favored staying in, lobstermen were fishing in some numbers at nearby Boothbay Harbor, South Bristol, and Christmas Cove, and of course mavericks had persisted in hauling all along the coast throughout the tie-ups. Early Thursday morning (August 8) about a hundred Casco Bay fishermen met informally in the parking lot at the Harris Company and, despite the Rockland vote, decided to go back to hauling immediately, with the price stuck at 32 and 30 cents for shedders. Within minutes there was a rush for bait at Brown's Wharf, fourteen boats had swung out toward the bay, and the small eateries in and around Commercial Street were deluged with orders for take-out lunches. "A lot of the boys are running out of money," said one man, and "the season is almost over," especially for the part-time summer men. The 1957 tie-ups were over, and the MLA stood defeated. The real drama, however, was only beginning.

Before the tie-up ended, Jack Willard had conferred with his brother and business associate, attorney Philip Willard, and discussed the threats of damage to boats and gear and harassment of men who wanted to fish for them. Other dealers, too, had passed on stories of retaliation against "scabs." Phil advised that "it should be the duty of the district attorney to restrain them [MLA lobstermen] from violence by a civil injunction."

The federal district attorney was an Eisenhower appointee, Peter Mills—a short, stocky, impish man with a cherubic smile and intent eyes, usually clad in a sports coat and tie. Like Mills, the Willards were Republicans. Mills's office was in downtown Portland not far from the wharves, so Phil Willard simply walked over and paid him a visit, immediately calling to Mills's attention Section 1 of the Sherman Anti-trust Act (pertaining to combinations or conspiracies in restraint of trade) and pointing out its relevance to the fishermen's tie-up and the role of the Maine Lobstermen's Association. What happened next was characteristically Maine.

Willard urged Mills to call Washington to have the Justice Depart-ment look into the events of the past weeks. Willard could see that Mills was hesitant about doing so, and shrewdly realized that Mills (on a tight budget and before the days of WATS lines) was mulling over not the propriety of such a call but, rather, the expense of a long-distance call. So Willard offered to pay for the call and, charging it to his num-ber, placed it for Mills.

Seldom have phone calls to Washington received such speedy re-sponse. Mills watched in amazement on August 9, 1957, the day the tie-up ended, as four Justice Department officials arrived, took over the grand jury room, and began conducting interviews with fishermen and lobster dealers. Was the U.S. Department of Justice really so concerned about what could hardly be regarded a vital industry? One theory was that the team of government lawyers, based in New York and eager to escape steamy Manhattan in the dog days of summer, seized this op-portunity for refreshment at the cool Maine shore. Another popular theory was that the robust chief of the team, John J. Galgay, who looked like he appreciated a good meal, had a strong personal interest in lob-sters. In any case, the government lawyers immediately went to work collecting information. On August 14, Leslie Dyer, who had talked already to the Justice Department lawyers in Portland, was served with a subpoena to appear before a grand jury at the federal courthouse on August 20 and to present documents and papers relating to the Maine Lobstermen's Association, especially any that concerned the price of live lobsters or the conditions affecting their hauling.

At 10 A.M. on August 20, Dyer appeared in Portland and presented the subpoenaed documents along with a plea from his lawyers for subsequent immunity from prosecution, but the judge ruled that his claim had no merit. The grand jury remained in session until early September, listening to more than forty witnesses who testified about all facets of the lobster industry. Peter Mills, accustomed to pinching dimes, was astounded at the resources available to the government men in material supplies, stenographic help, and cash.

Meanwhile, dazed lobster fishermen paraded in and out of the grand jury room. One Portland-area fisherman, neatly dressed in a light suit, white shirt and bow tie, and with a crew cut and receding hairline, told of MLA threats and of actually having had more than a hundred dollars worth of traps cut away for not cooperating. Some, like Bernard Johnson, came to Portland and just sat in an anteroom for several hours, never speaking to anyone. Others, who did testify, emerged looking confused and told reporters, "I don't know a thing" or "I don't know why I'm here." Before coming to Portland some of the fishermen had been visited by a pair of government lawyers and had been engaged in friendly conversation. Robert Waddle of Quahog Bay near Harpswell, an ex-Marine and MLA activist, recalled acting like "melba milk toast and [saying] what they wanted me to say." Some of the MLA men came to regret having talked freely in front of stenographers and the grand jury, out of a trusting indiscretion born partly of fear and partly of an ignorance of legal procedures. In a later conversation with the government lawyers, the MLA fisherman Myles O'Reilly pointedly referred to the grand jury room as "that little room where you tried to brainwash us."

On September 5, dealers, too, trooped before the grand jury: five from Rockland, four of them dapper in dark suits and white shirts and the fifth with a light suit and loud tie; Harold Look was represented by his son, Harold Jr. Dealers' firms also, including the Willard-Daggett and Benson Seafood companies, received subpoenas to submit their records to the grand jury. Meanwhile, some dealers were reported to have dropped the price for shedder lobsters below 30 cents, to 28 and even 25 cents, because dealers were anticipating the impact of a new size law on January 1, and some of the lobsters they were buying now would supposedly not be big enough to be legal after that date.

Les Dyer was talking not only to the grand jury and his lawyer friends during this period, but also to the newspapers, and he was venting a good deal of the association's anger at the dealers. That anger, already high when the tie-up fizzled out, intensified as the federal government entered the scene. Dyer announced moves under way to form a large co-op. "We've outgrown the present system of depending on dealers to do our marketing for us." He believed that lobstermen needed to develop permanent alternatives to the dealers' price-cutting as a way of handling the annual glut. He also raised questions about dealers' recent tactics of manipulating the supply of bait in order to deny it to fishermen who chose not to sell to them. He charged, too, that some dealers owned or claimed to own various offshore islands and sought to restrict fishing around those places or to charge fishermen fees for fishing those waters (by paying them lower prices). In Casco Bay, the name Willard kept coming up in connection with such accusations.

On October 15, 1957, the U.S. government indicted the MLA and Leslie Dyer Jr. for conspiracy "to fix, stabilize and maintain the prices for live Maine lobsters sold by MLA member and non-member lobstermen to lobster dealers, in unreasonable restraint of . . . interstate trade and commerce in live Maine lobsters, in violation of Section 1 of the Act of Congress of July 2, 1890, entitled 'An Act to protect trade and commerce against unlawful restraints and monopolies' . . . commonly known as the Sherman Act." The Sherman Antitrust Act had emerged from the nation's first anxious moments over the formation of large industrial and capital combines at the end of the nineteenth century. While used subsequently to attack monopoly, oligopoly, and price-fixing among corporate giants, it had not really slowed the growth of big business. Other ironies followed, especially the use of the act against striking laborers to deter the formation of labor unions. But employing the Sherman Act against a group of men who were quint-essentially small businessmen-craftsmen-entrepreneurs was an even greater irony, since it was the nineteenth century's ideal of the small producer that the law was in part intended to protect.

The indictments sent shock waves through the ranks of lobster fishermen, who normally want nothing to do with the law and who prefer personal negotiations. Some dealers played upon the credulity of some lobstermen by spreading rumors that they faced fines, possible imprisonment, or even loss of their boats. Several "scairt" fishermen immediately took their boats out of the water and hid them away from home; a few towed them on trailers to inland lakes, out of reach of the government.

Leslie Dyer, Alan Grossman, and their friends could hardly have been surprised by the indictments. But the government tacked on a shocking announcement. Also indicted were seven Portland-area lobster dealers, including Willard-Daggett and Benson, for having conspired to fix the price of lobsters and for inducing other dealers to join in their combination. Most of the dealers had little to say, though one called it a "complete surprise," and Jack Willard said he thought the charges "ridiculous." The dealers, of course, pleaded innocent.

In typical hardheaded Yankee fashion, one isolated fisherman, on hearing that the government had charged lobstermen with trying to get higher prices for their catch, asked: "What's wrong with that?" Senator Frederick G. Payne, Republican, said he was "shocked" at the indictments and said that if there had been wrongdoing, then a warning would have sufficed instead of government "persecution." Like many other observers, Payne pointed to the "increasing flood" of Canadian lobsters into Maine markets and urged the government to change its trade policies. Canadian lobsters were no figment of the imagination. During July, Herbert McIntire, a Small Point dealer, had written a letter to Portland's newspaper, reporting that "last week I called every buyer that I have ever sold to in trying to sell the new shell Maine lobster and I got the same answer from them all. 'We don't want new shell Maine lobsters as we are getting old shell Canadians, all we want.' "

Public opinion ran strongly in favor of the lobstermen and against the dealers and the federal government. Except for the Portland *Telegram and Herald,* newspapers in Maine and Boston sided with the fishermen. The Boston *Herald*'s editorials sounded a theme common to several: Why were fishermen any different from farmers or trade unions? The government tells farmers to stop growing corn to let prices rise, and New York dairy farmers strike with impunity, whitening the highways with dumped milk and battling nonstriking farmers. "Quotas and acreage controls on land farmers have become a familiar part of American agrarianism. But when the sea farmers attempt to do something of the same, the anti-trust division of the Justice Department clamps down on them. Seems it's a laissez-faire economy—as long as the laissez-fairing is what the government says."

The *Maine Coast Fisherman* harshly criticized the dealers and accused them of wanting to break the lobstermen's association. They should have been spending their time finding new markets, but they preferred "to curtail production and thereby control it. They wish to keep on using the lobster industry as their own crap game. They'd rather be speculators than merchandisers." Morris Helioff, a Rockland dealer who had begun his career in New York's Fulton Fish Market, echoed this point in proposing a lobster exchange, one benefit of which would to prevent the "jockeying" of prices by big dealers. Another Rockland dealer, who preferred to remain anonymous, told the Rockland *Courier-Gazette* that ill will was spread by dealers who "take it on themselves 'willy-nilly' to set prices and create artificial shortages and gluts when there is no shortage nor surplus."

In defense of dealers, Chester R. Brown, a Boothbay wholesaler in business for twenty-five years, blamed the Canadian influx, swollen that year by a fifteen-day extension of Newfoundland's season and a big catch. Brown claimed that in the past year he had grossed 10 percent and netted 1 percent on $400,000 worth of business. He enjoyed, he said, only a 10 cent spread between his buying and selling price, half of which went to subdealers who buy from fishermen and sell to him. He estimated that it cost him about 5 cents a pound to handle lobsters from the time they left the subdealers until he delivered them to other buyers at 40 cents a pound. Brown figured that his costs plus losses of lobsters in transit or in holding tanks caused his wholesale operation to break even, and that he made his money from sales to restaurants and hotels.

Despite manifest public sympathy for the fishermen, the Justice Department's New York team pressed on with its prosecution. On December 3, lawyers for Dyer and the MLA argued before U.S. District Court Judge Edward Gignoux that the indictments should be dismissed, but on December 21 the judge denied the motions. Accordingly, on December 27, both Dyer and the MLA were arraigned (separately) before Gignoux and entered pleas of not guilty. Postponed twice, the trial would not begin until May 19, 1958, in part because the lead government counsel, John Galgay, suffered from stomach ulcers. Lobstermen who recall the 1958 trial retain vivid memories of Galgay "popping Tums" in the courthouse corridors. The judge may also have wanted to wait until winter ended so that witnesses traveling from Down East could avoid bad weather. In any case, the delay gave the MLA time to raise money for its defense.

Earlier, in October, Dyer had admitted at an MLA meeting that only fifteen hundred fishermen had paid dues during the past year, and the organization's indictment did not help matters. Some fishermen nevertheless rallied to the MLA. Shortly after the October meeting, Dyer received a letter from Elbridge G. Simmons of Swan's Island, enclosing his five dollars in dues and expressing the wish to be enrolled in an organization the government had indicted "for trying to get a decent living for its members." The hard-core MLA men in fact became increasingly feisty, with groups meeting after the arraignments and passing resolutions that defiantly promised to fight the government. On February 5 a large assembly of MLA delegates met in Rockland's GAR Hall and voted to contest the charges. They would raise money for their defense from dues, donations, suppers, and dances, and on the spot collected "several hundred dollars."

Soon after the usual group of storytellers had their feet up around the potbellied stove in Cliff Island's only store, it hit someone that a quorum of the local fire department was present. They called a meeting and voted fifty dollars from the Firemen's Relief Fund to go to the "lobstermen's defense fund." That afternoon, the island's Mothers' Club contributed another fifty dollars.

When fishermen meet on the water and want to take a break, they tie their boats together, drink coffee, and gab—such encounters are known as mug-ups. Along the Maine coast, supporters of the lobstermen that winter and spring began to organize benefit dinners which they called "Mug-Ups." The most publicized was held at Owl's Head near Rockland, organized by the Ladies' Grange and led by a fisherman's wife, Elena Fredette, a pretty and spirited brunette who also fired off angry letters to unfriendly newspapers. The Owl's Head folk served three shifts of dinner in a school auditorium seating two hundred, and in about two hours dispensed 35 pounds of spaghetti, 10 gallons of sauce, 20 pounds of hamburger, 23 pots of baked beans, 24 brown breads, 1,000 rolls, 650 biscuits, 70 pounds of cabbage, 25 molded salads, 35 cakes, and uncounted gallons of coffee and milk.

So it went through the winter. Baked bean and spaghetti suppers, dances and raffles—all to raise money to help small, independent fishermen pay their legal-defense costs for prosecution under the Sherman Antitrust Act. No one could recall one of America's giant corporations holding such events for such a purpose.

3 THE TRIAL BEGINS

"If you'd asked me the right questions, I'd a-told you
more."

—Myles L. "Mike" O'Reilly Jr.

t about eight in the morning the white lobster boat left its
mooring at Springett's on the northeast side of the island and
headed south and west to a small wharf in Coleman's Cove.
Waiting there was Albion Miller, a tall, fair-skinned fisherman with a
twinkle in his blue eyes. Snatches of morning fog still clung to the
water on a cool spring day that promised sunny skies in the afternoon.
The *Ernie B,* a Hamilton-style thirty-two-footer with a 120 Nauberg
engine, then rounded the evergreen spear of Deer Point at the island's southwest end and made way on a rising tide toward Portland's
wharves some five miles away. At the wheel stood Alger Burgess, accompanied by his wife, Shirley, the boat's fifteen-year-old namesake,
Miller, and Ralph Small, a broad-shouldered, low-browed fisherman
who, because he had served a brief term as an MLA delegate, looked
worried. It was Monday, May 19, 1958, the first day of *United States of
America* v. *Maine Lobstermen's Association and Leslie C. Dyer.*

While Shirley chatted with Albion and Ralph, Alger's own
thoughts brought wry smiles to his face as he contemplated the charge

of criminal conspiracy against the fishermen. He entertained no doubt that the dealers had fixed the goddamn price, they always had. For the U.S. government to equate the MLA's tie-up with Willard's and the dealers' habitual price-fixing was both unfair and ridiculous. A World War II veteran of the Coast Guard, Alger had fished full-time since the war from Chebeague Island where he had come as an outsider (from Peaks Island in Portland harbor) after marrying one of the Ross clan, whose roots went back to the island's late-eighteenth-century settlement. In his prime at age forty, five feet nine inches tall, barrel-chested and stocky, with his once-blond hair turning brown, Alger looked strong and tough. He had evolved into a natural leader of the island fishermen because he was thoughtful, fair, and a "good talker" who often saw through to the heart of a matter. Although his father had not been a fisherman, but skippered Portland's fireboat, Alger became an excellent "lobstercatcher," to use his preferred word, a skill he passed on.

During these years Alger and Shirley were raising three children (Ernie was the oldest) and thus were active in church (Chebeague Island Methodist) and youth affairs. They were also drawn to Edmund Muskie's rejuvenation of Maine's Democratic Party. In 1958 Shirley became the island postmaster, a job she would hold for roughly three decades. Alger also cared about the lobster fishery. He fished three hundred traps at peak season, a normal "gang" then. In twenty years that amount of gear would pale by comparison to the mob of traps lobstermen would haul, but Alger already believed that trap limits made sense. He had also trekked to Augusta with other lobstercatchers to lobby the legislature to eliminate the licensing of "summer dubbers" and to restrict the fishery to men who made their living principally from lobsters.

Alger nestled the *Ernie B* into Brown's Wharf in the heart of the Portland waterfront, where other lobster boats were tying up. The waterfront still bristled with pilings, spars, masts, and booms, and its many brick buildings retained an almost nineteenth-century flavor. But like other East Coast cities, the port had endured a long, slow decline in the twentieth century, briefly halted by the war, and many of the older structures stood idle and decaying.

Alger's crew headed up across Commercial Street to "Theodore's," a storefront lunchroom. There they sat, smoked, drank coffee, and ate doughnuts and muffins before walking a short distance uphill to the federal courthouse. Alger would not testify until Thursday, but they would come in every day that week to watch the proceedings and especially, as the trial wore on, to catch the show: the Maine lobster-catchers, wrapping themselves in coastal patois for protective cover, matching wits with the "slick talkers" from New York, leading them verbally on a chase across the waters and around the islands of Casco Bay through hours of evasive testimony.

The federal courthouse stood stolidly two blocks up a small hill from Commercial Street. Built in 1911 of Maine granite and masonry, its three-storied plain visage still conveys authority. Except for a 1932 extension, it looked in 1958 essentially as it did when constructed. Its spacious, high-ceiling courtroom remained ornate and graceful, yet to the ordinary fisherman must have seemed intimidating. Entering from the rear, you saw five enormous windows along the wall to the right, a soaring curved ceiling hung with two chandeliers, and behind the judge's bench a back wall, recessed in the middle and lined with portraits, decorative Greek columns, and sconces. The bench was bracketed by globe lamps sitting on long stems, and oriental rugs partly covered a polished floor between the bench and tables that were reserved for attorneys and court personnel. The witness box stood immediately to the left of the bench, and beyond it on the left wall was a movable jury box furnished with sturdy oak chairs, a velvet rope strung across its front. On the left wall sat the bailiff's box between two doors. In the middle was a large section for spectators, at the front of which reporters sat. At once elegant and rustic, more than a hint of antiquity attached itself, appropriately, to this the oldest sitting federal court in the United States.

The presiding judge, on the other hand, was at the time of his appointment in 1957 the youngest ever to hold a U.S. district court seat. But forty-one-year-old Edward T. Gignoux quickly established himself as a presence as formidable as the venerable building he commanded. If a Hollywood mogul had called central casting and ordered a cross between Gary Cooper and Ralph Bellamy, Gignoux could have filled the role. Tall, ruggedly handsome, self-confident, and blessed with a deep, resonant voice, Gignoux seemed the very essence of a judge—and he was charming, articulate, and intelligent. More than one associate characterized him as "Lincolnesque."

He was born in Portland in 1916, his father Fred T. Gignoux the proprietor of a successful ship chandlery. His "patrician manner" had been honed at St. George's, a prep school for the rich in Newport, Rhode Island, and then at Harvard University. Academic honors followed him to Harvard Law School, where he edited the *Law Review,* and from which he was graduated in 1940. Gignoux began his career in Buffalo, New York, then moved to Washington, D.C., and by 1942 he was in the U.S. Army. During a three-year tour in the Southwest Pacific with the First Cavalry, he rose to major and received the Legion of Merit and the Bronze Star. After the war, he came back to Portland seeking the healing powers of his beloved Maine coast as he recuperated from a wartime illness. During law school Gignoux had already married well—Hildegard Schuyler Thaxter, a beauty of impeccable Maine lineage and the daughter of a state supreme court justice. Soon he joined a prestigious Portland law firm and devoted himself to his career and to raising a family.

From a Republican background, Gignoux was not particularly partisan. He did the kinds of things elite Republicans often do: nonprofit volunteer work for charities, service on the chamber of commerce and as assistant corporation counsel for Portland, and two terms on the city council (1949–55). Then he got lucky. Maine's Southern Federal District judicial seat opened, and Maine's two U.S. senators, Frederick Payne and Margaret Chase Smith, both submitted lists of names to the Eisenhower administration. The story, still current in Portland's legal community, was that Gignoux's was the only name on both lists, and so he emerged as the compromise candidate.

The antitrust "lobster trial" came at the beginning of what would be a distinguished career. Several times Gignoux was tapped to handle controversial or sensitive cases: the 1973 contempt retrial of the 1968 "Chicago Seven" war protesters; the 1983 bribery-contempt trial of the African-American U.S. district judge Alcee Hastings of Miami. In the 1970s, Gignoux also presided over the attempt by two Maine Indian tribes to recover 10 million acres from the state under a 1790 law. Gignoux made history by finding the statute legal, resulting in a settlement by which the federal government gave the Penobscot and Passamaquoddy tribes $27 million and $54.5 million, respectively, in payment for 300,000 acres. By 1988, shortly before his retirement, the stone building on Federal Street would be renamed the Edward Thaxter Gignoux Courthouse, in a ceremony at which the judge's once sonorous voice was silenced by throat cancer.

Though he was a newly minted judge, Gignoux brought to the MLA trial a familiarity both with the lobster industry and with Dyer and Grossman. In 1953, counsel Gignoux had represented the North Atlantic Lobster Institute (NALI), a dealer group, at legislative hearings in Augusta concerning a NALI-sponsored bill to increase the minimum legal length of Maine lobsters to three and three-sixteenth inches, the same as in Massachusetts, where, the dealers argued, more than 60 percent of Maine's catch was sent to market. Opposing the measure was a delegation of a hundred or so fishermen headed by Leslie Dyer and Alan Grossman. (It was while testifying against the increase that Dyer made his "hog on ice" remark.) In opposition Gignoux argued that the change would make the Maine lobster "a more marketable commodity, increasing the dollar return to both dealers and fishermen." Five years later, the continuing struggle between fishermen and dealers over "the dollar return" brought Gignoux, Dyer, and Grossman together again.

Alan Grossman now sat at the attorneys' table across from Gignoux's bench, ready for combat, his populist sensibilities and sense of fair play outraged by what he regarded as an excessive show of punitive force against hardworking men of modest means. Didn't the U.S. Department of Justice, he wondered, have better things to do than to come to Maine and prosecute fishermen? Grossman would represent the MLA, and Stanley Tupper would represent Les Dyer. Tall, blond, with a crew cut and looking younger than his thirty-seven years, Tupper was a Boothbay Harbor attorney whose advocacy of fishermen would lead him into politics. He had just finished a four-year stint as commissioner of fisheries and, later, as a liberal Republican opposed to the presidential nomination of the conservative Barry Goldwater, he would be elected to Congress in a state famed for its political independence. Tactful, politic, and soft-spoken, Tupper would handle some of the defense's courtroom work, but Grossman took on the lion's share of argument for the defense. Two well-connected and ambitious young Portland lawyers, Philip F. Chapman Jr. and Milton A. Nixon, also received billing as defense counsel, but played minimal roles.

Grossman and Tupper were assisted mainly by Grossman's junior associate from Rockland, John L. Knight, a ferret of a man who did the typing, digging, and other hard labor for the defense. Small, intense, with large dark glasses on an elfin head topped with smoothly combed brown hair, Knight had just graduated from Boston's Suffolk Law School and was working in Grossman's office while also serving his first term in the Maine legislature. A local Irish-Catholic who had gone from high school in 1943 into the wartime maritime service, Knight, an adopted child, adored his mentor Grossman and would stay up into the early morning hours typing motions.

Across from the defense sat an imposing array of legal artillery on behalf of the United States. On the first day, the local D.A., Peter Mills, was in court, joined by Richard B. O'Donnell, chief of the Justice Department's Antitrust Division. Four other antitrust lawyers, however, who Mills called "the platoon from New York," actually handled the courtroom work. John J. Galgay led the squad, a witty, heavy-set, ruddy-faced Irish-Catholic, who had been born forty years ago in Cambridge, Massachusetts, on the other side of the Charles River from Alan Grossman. The second of seven children, Galgay as a youth worked in the family's Cambridge flower shop. After high school he entered Northeastern Law School and, like many other upwardly mobile Irish-Catholic youth in Boston, attended an elocution school. Apprenticing briefly for a couple of downtown Boston firms, in 1941 Galgay married a recent graduate of a local Catholic college who was the daughter of a Cambridge city official. Galgay served a brief stint in the Army during the war, then returned to private practice and to fathering his own family of seven (the last child was born during the lobster trial). In 1948 he went to work for the Justice Department in Boston, but in 1954 his office was consolidated with New York City's and the family quickly followed his career to the New York suburbs.

Contrary to speculation, Galgay did not relish the crustacean as a meal, but his wife, Corinne, did, and on weekend visits to his family in

New York, Galgay carried cartons of iced live lobster to his pregnant wife. Peter Mills, who was almost as perplexed as Alan Grossman about why the government had decided to devote such lavish resources to this case, believed that Galgay & Co. were looking to win feathers for their caps. Yet Galgay confided to one colleague at the outset that he believed the government actually had only an even or worse chance of getting a conviction from a Maine jury.

Second in command to Galgay was another Boston-area product, thirty-seven-year-old Alan L. Lewis, a graduate of Harvard College (1942) and, after a wartime interruption, the Boston University School of Law (1949). Short, with dark hair and glasses, Lewis looked and sounded lawyerly—crisp, businesslike, and with a deep, authoritative voice. The two junior members of the government team presented a contrast in regional and cultural origins. Philip Bloom, a kosher-keeping Jew from the New York area, would turn twenty-eight in the course of the trial, and saw himself as "low man on the totem pole." He had gone into government service soon after getting his undergraduate and law degrees from Columbia and, after driving his new red-and-white Plymouth to Portland from New York, fell in love with the Maine coast.

But Bloom's first sight of a lobster was a jolting experience: "ugliest thing I'd ever seen." He and Joe F. Nowlin, the other junior man, who hailed from lobster-barren Arkansas, would ask each other: "Who is the strongest, bravest guy in the world?" The answer: "The one with the courage to be the first to eat a lobster." Joe Nowlin was thirty-four and a decade away from Arkansas State Teachers College and the University of Alabama Law School. Squarish in build, with dark glasses and a genial expression, Nowlin, said one of his colleagues, "looked like a penguin with a Southern accent."

The remaining characters who would be on stage throughout the entire courtroom drama were the jury, two court reporters, and the bailiff and crier John Higgins. "Johnny" Higgins, at the beginning of a long career during which he became a devoted servant of Gignoux (who had appointed him), was a handsome, young, blue-eyed Irishman of medium height and judicial appearance endowed with a booming baritone voice. When he trumpeted the entrance of Gignoux and called the assemblage to order, it seemed that any fisherman arriving late at the wharves, blocks below, might have heard him.

Harry Derry was court reporter and, like Higgins, had started work shortly after Gignoux's appointment just months before. This tall, thin, quiet young man (not yet twenty-seven), clerkish in a proper white shirt and tie, faded into the background quickly during his shifts on the stenotype machine. His relief reporter, however, hardly ever went unnoticed. Irene Manoogian (later Arabian) was a twenty-eight-year-old, black-haired, dark-eyed stunner, tall and well proportioned, with sparkling eyes and a gorgeous smile. Based in Boston, and already a veteran of eight years of court reporting, Arabian had been free-lancing for the past four years, and she and Galgay had worked together in Boston. Galgay, coming to Portland so suddenly from New York, had requested Irene and another Boston stenographer for the grand jury hearings, and the competent, workaholic Arabian stayed on for the trial to assist Derry. At times, a fisherman on the witness stand would need to have a question repeated, because his eyes had wandered in Irene's direction. She and Derry worked in shifts of twenty minutes of verbatim recording. On one of Derry's stints Irene failed to relieve him on time and he grew weary. Finally, a break in the trial allowed Derry to search for Irene. He found her in an office down the hall doing her best to keep a desk between herself and a booted, red-faced fisherman who was cooing, "You're a sweetie and I'm going to get you."

On the first day, an extraordinary number of potential jurors—the jury panel—had assembled for questioning and winnowing by judge and counsel. Although newspaper reports of the trial had sparked enormous interest, when the judge asked how many had heard or read anything about the case, only a half-dozen raised their hands. This astonished Peter Mills, who quickly concluded that these citizens probably knew about the case and wanted to serve. Judge Gignoux began with a brief civics lesson on the importance of jury duty, explaining court procedures and their duty to be the final arbiter of contested facts. He would decide the law. He asked them to avoid newspaper, radio, and television accounts of the trial, telling them that those who served as jurors would actually know more of "what has actually transpired" than those following events in the news media. Gignoux then weeded out jurors principally on the basis of any connection to the fishing industry. When the process of questioning, challenges, and drawing was complete, the jury consisted of a heavily inland and older group, a majority of whom were retirees. Gignoux selected Orlando C. Woodman, a sixty-four-year-old superintendent of schools in Gardiner, to be foreman. Woodman, just under five feet eleven inches and weighing 200 pounds, was an energetic, pleasant-looking man of almost puckish demeanor, easy to like, and someone who relished being foreman. After another peptalk, Gignoux reminded the jury that court would convene each morning at 9:30 and run until 12 noon, with a midmorning recess, then reconvene at 1:30 and go until 4:00 P.M., with a midafternoon recess. Jurors would get long week-ends, Friday through Sunday.

On reconvening that first afternoon, the clerk immediately read the full indictment against the MLA and Leslie Dyer, charging them with "a combination and conspiracy to fix, stabilize and maintain the prices for live Maine lobsters sold by both MLA member and non-member lobstermen to lobster dealers, in unreasonable restraint of . . . interstate trade and commerce . . . in violation of Section 1 of the Act of Congress of July 2, 1890, . . . commonly known as the Sherman Act." The judge cautioned the jury that what it had heard was simply an accusation and not proof of wrongdoing. John Galgay then rose for the prosecution.

Galgay began slowly, as if taking the jurors into his confidence. He stressed that MLA members, some two thousand of Maine's six thousand licensed lobstermen, consisted of independent fishermen who did not catch or market lobsters collectively in any way, thus exempting them from immunity to antitrust laws under a fisheries cooperative law. He described the broad contours of the lobster industry and the need to dispose of lobsters within about seventy-two hours—instead of five to seven days—during "shedder" season. There was no need to dwell, however, "on the general consumer acceptance of Maine live lobsters throughout the entire country for, as everyone knows, it is widely regarded as a seafood delicacy."

The government, said Galgay, saw the MLA's actions as a typical "per se" violation of the Sherman Act, meaning that it simply needed to prove a price-fixing agreement. "This means that you need not, in fact you must not, inquire or determine *whether the price fixed was*

a fair price or an unfair price, a good price or a bad price; the mere
fact that prices were fixed by agreement in and of itself constitutes a
violation." Having pronounced the morality of the fishermen's position as irrelevant, Galgay now boldly addressed the public sympathy
they enjoyed.

"There has been a good deal of irresponsible talk in the public
press and on radio and T.V. that the Maine lobster fisherman has
been discriminated against or is being prosecuted unjustly for conduct
which the farmer or laborer would not be prosecuted. . . . Now this
is perfect nonsense." The Sherman Act, he avowed, was a charter of
economic freedom, with certain exemptions, each with specific limita-
tions. Potato farmers in Aroostook County had established cooperatives under the "agricultural cooperative" exemption, as had some
poultry farmers. Indeed, some lobster fishermen had formed co-ops
under the Fisheries Cooperatives Act. But the MLA, for reasons best
known to themselves, chose to ignore this legal course of action.

The government would show, said Galgay, that the MLA at various
meetings during 1957 had decided on price-fixing. The government
would also prove that an MLA meeting of delegates and executive
council on July 19, 1957, unanimously decided that MLA members
would stop production until a minimum price of 35 cents a pound was
established for shedders along the entire coast. Delegates then returned
home and told MLA members and nonmember fishermen of the decision, using meetings in the local library or hall to pass along the word.
Further, MLA members then "patrolled the waters" inducing all to go
ashore and, Galgay intoned, hinting at coercion, "agreed to do *everything possible* to stop non-members from hauling in order that their
illegal scheme might be successful."

When Galgay finished, the defendants declined to make an opening statement, so the government began to call its witnesses, beginning
with their own colleague, Philip Bloom, who entered fifty-three MLA
documents into evidence. Alan Grossman then sprang forward and
subjected Bloom to spirited cross-examination, whose purpose was
not always clear, but certainly served notice to Galgay & Co. that they
would be challenged at every point. Grossman lost no time in crossing
swords with "Brother Galgay" over the minutest detail. His larger
point, not supported by the judge, was that the documents brought in

by Dyer and now given as evidence were Dyer's own, and not official MLA records.

After a midafternoon recess, the government called two fisheries experts. Galgay had hoped to get the defense to agree to government figures regarding the volume of lobstercatching and marketing over the past two years, and thus to dispense with testimony, but Grossman would not allow it. So David McKown, of West Boothbay, a state-fishing market specialist, took the stand, followed by his good friend and colleague Louis Robert Cates, of Rockland, who like McKown was a statistician for the Department of Sea and Shore Fisheries. Between them, McKown and Cates gathered data for the eastern and western halves of the Maine coast, and the two could hardly fail to inspire confidence in the government's case.

The fifty-eight-year-old McKown was a handsome man, stocky, with white hair, blue eyes behind glasses, a clear speaking voice, and an aura of integrity combined with a ready smile. Cates, in his early sixties, also wore glasses; he had a fair complexion, brown hair, and a crisp, authoritative voice, and he prided himself on his natty ward-robe. Their reassuring presences, however, gained them no reprieve from Alan Grossman's catlike scrutiny. The defense objected that the information from Cates's and McKown's testimony was "remote," but Gignoux overruled him. Grossman was able to reveal, however, that the prices McKown used to determine the value of lobster landings came wholly from buyers or dealers and were never checked with fishermen. Grossman also raised the possibility that dealers could buy, say, fifty thousand pounds of Canadian lobsters and report them as Maine lobsters. Though illegal, there was no way to check on such practices.

Ironically, the jury heard twice—and from the government—data on total pounds landed and on their value for 1956 and 1957 that might have given any thoughtful observer an understanding of the lobster-men's discontent: 20,572,000 lobsters at $9,100,000 in 1956, against 24,402,000 lobsters at a lesser value of $8,954,000 in 1957.

The second day of the trial began with the government drawing descriptions of the lobster trade from two dealers, Edward C. Palmer and Donald E. Barnes. The middle-aged Palmer, dark and heavy, had been in the seafood business for thirty-four years and had worked his way up to ownership of a medium-size lobster company. Barnes's future as a dealer, wholesaler, and seafood speculator lay before him. Then in his twenties, the baby-faced Barnes had a twinkle in his eye and a charming manner. He had begun his Sea Breeze Lobster Company, the smallest in Portland, just four years ago. Neither man wanted to be there, nor did either one relish the role of government witness. They would need to work with the fishermen after the trial was over. The judge needed to ask each man several times to keep up his voice. In addition, of course, dealers habitually disliked divulging information about their businesses.

During the rather undramatic testimony of first Palmer and then Barnes, however, the defense explored a line of questioning that the judge disallowed and, in so doing, effectively deprived them of an argument. Palmer told Galgay that in 1957 he grossed about $300,000 and that he was supplied by about thirty local fishermen. Some 75 percent of his lobsters went out of state, primarily to concerns at New York's Fulton Fish Market. He shipped lobsters by refrigerator truck, in twenty-five- and fifty-pound barrels, held in racks and covered with ice. Successful transport depended on many things, including the lobsters' initial condition, the season, and the time in transit. Hard-shell lobsters could last a month in his storage tanks; shedder lobsters needed to reach the consumer in two or three days.

Stan Tupper rose to cross-examine Palmer and calmly plunged into an area that the prosecution would quickly protest. Tupper asked Palmer if he belonged to an association? "Maine Fisheries Association—Associated Fisheries of Maine, that's what it is." Tupper then asked in his businesslike way: "Mr. Palmer, could you tell the Court, and again briefly, how you set the price of lobsters each morning?" Galgay objected, and Tupper asked for a conference at the bench, out of hearing of the jury.

Tupper: "I think it's in order, your Honor, to bring out in our case that this alleged conspiracy was in fact a defense mechanism, and I think our whole line of questioning may depend on admitting some of that." Knowing that a critical point had surfaced, not just Galgay but his chief, Richard O'Donnell, moved swiftly to the bench: "He's going into the wholesale price [*sic*], your Honor, and this is the fishermen's case. He's not talking about dealers' prices." Judge: "If the Court understands the applicable law correctly, if the Government establishes [the existence of] a price-fixing agreement, the purpose of the agreement and the moral justification it might have had—in fact, the price may have been a fair one, it's completely immaterial. Is that correct?" Galgay: "Yes, your Honor." (Of course Gignoux was supposed to be the "final arbiter" of the law, but given his lack of experience with antitrust cases, he turned for confirmation of his own thinking to the government experts, hardly impartial observers.) Judge: "Under these circumstances, the Court cannot see how it is material to show that any price-fixing agreement was a defense mechanism."

And that was it. After offering the defense the opportunity later to explore dealers' prices or price-setting with their own witnesses, the judge ended the bench conference—and any grounds for an effective defense.

Grossman began his examination of Barnes by trying to get the jury to understand that part of the summer "glut" was caused by dealers importing Canadian lobsters. Barnes had already said that he bought some of his lobsters from other dealers. Did he know whether those lobsters were Canadian or Maine lobsters? "I believe they're all Maine lobsters." "How do you know?" "I can tell by the look of them." "And what is the look that led you to believe that a certain lobster is a Maine lobster and not a Canadian, or a Canadian and not a Maine lobster?" The lawyers on both sides grinned, but Barnes parried Grossman nicely.

"Anyone that's been been dealing with them long enough, they have a certain color and a certain—you can tell by the shell. Most of these lobsters that I've bought from other dealers . . . are shedders. Anyone in the lobster business can tell the difference." Barnes added that he bought few hard shells and when he did, he sold them directly to one buyer.

Then Grossman tried to revive the line of attack that the judge had just squelched. "Did you meet with other lobster dealers during the month of June, July and August last year?" Lewis objected, of course, and Gignoux asked counsel to come to the bench, where he asked Grossman if he was renewing Tupper's failed tack. Gignoux: "The Court has ruled that [it] will not permit the introduction . . . of any alleged conspiracy or a combination between the dealers. . . . If counsel has any proper basis for inquiring along this line, the Court will appreciate hearing it." Grossman replied that "if the lobster fishermen were forced by the actions of others to try to stop an illegal conspiracy, which we maintain they did, we say that that evidence is admissible. Another thing I'm trying to show . . . that there is such a thing as bait being an important issue as to whether or not the supply of lobsters drops or increases. If there was no bait, there's a possibility that that might have caused a slowdown." The judge said that inquiry about bait would be proper, but he repeated his ruling that the purpose of a price-fixing agreement is "completely immaterial." Again he checked with the prosecution as to whether his understanding of the law was correct, and O'Donnell concurred: "There is no defense."

The game was lost, but Grossman wasn't through. "If the dealers requested the fishermen to stop fishing because there was a glut, we can't go into that either?" No, said Gignoux. Grossman then repeated his desire to show both a dealers' conspiracy regarding price and a bait conspiracy, leading the judge to repeat his bar against "any effort to inject into this case the related case which is brought against the lobster dealers pending before this court." The defense counsel grimly returned to their seats.

Grossman still believed he could get something out of Barnes, however, and so he pursued the matter of bait. Though "Barnes's" fishermen bought bait from a local company, Barnes did sell some bait to fishermen. Did he, Grossman wanted to know, sell bait to any fisherman who sold his catch to another dealer? Barnes deflated Grossman's tack: "I sold bait to fishermen that didn't sell me lobsters." But if bait was in short supply, "my own fishermen would come first." Onlookers and especially fishermen chuckled at what came next. "Was there any complaint last summer to you that the price of bait was too high?" Barnes: "Ever since I've handled bait, I've always had complaints of it being too high."

Soon after, court adjourned for morning recess.

The government next called the first lobsterman witness, Robert E. Waddle of Brunswick, but as soon as Galgay began his questioning, Grossman interrupted with an objection that "the witness should be informed as to his right before he answers any questions in this hearing." Galgay, bristling, called this "a ridiculous assertion on the part of Brother Grossman." He should know, Galgay continued, of the section of antitrust law which provides immunity for a witness subpoenaed by the court. "I might further add, your Honor, that Mr. Grossman has been advising practically every Government witness erroneously in this regard." Gignoux said his reading of the law concurred with Galgay's.

Grossman: "May I be heard? I might be ridiculous [drawing out the word for emphasis], as my *New York lawyer* has explained to the Court, but I do say we have a statute in the State of Maine that provides for certain penalties under a section similar to the Government's Sherman Antitrust Act." Was "my learned brother" claiming there is immunity in state courts for this man? "Is that what he has been telling the witnesses?" Galgay: "I haven't been telling the witnesses anything, your Honor. It is Mr. Grossman who has hampered the progress of this case."

Gignoux intervened. He recognized that in their zeal, counsel might "exceed the normal bounds of courtesy," yet he requested that the lawyers refrain from improper comments about one another. He thereupon excused the jury and invited counsel into his chambers for discussion on the record. Inside, he repeated his strong view that inappropriate comments had been made by both sides, and in his most engaging manner he added that "the Court is certain that counsel do not really mean it."

In a conference that straddled the lunch hour, Grossman made his stand on a section of Maine law from the 1954 statutes book that was indeed similar to federal antitrust law. Joe Nowlin stated the prosecution's position that a witness testifying in federal court could not claim immunity under the Fifth Amendment based on a possible violation of state law. Indeed, if a witness should in the course of testifying "reveal that he has committed murder, for example, or larceny or any crime that you wish to conceive under state law, he does not have a privilege against incriminating himself." Conversely, argued Nowlin, a witness before a state court is compelled to answer a question that might reveal he has violated a federal law. The judge then advised the parties that several cases called to his attention (by his young law clerk, Ralph

Lancaster) supported the government's contention that a witness could not refuse to testify on the grounds offered by Grossman.

After lunch Gignoux announced that he had done "a little research during the noon recess." He now ruled confidently that any claim against self-incrimination under the Fifth Amendment must be raised by the witness himself, and this witness had not done so. Gignoux then deftly moved the conference to deal with the documents that the government wished to enter as evidence. After protracted discussion, with Grossman battling every step, the MLA documents and Dyer's meeting records were admitted. Finally, Gignoux returned to Grossman's request, just before the recess, that Robert Waddle be instructed as to his rights. "The request is denied."

Court resumed with Galgay's questioning of Robert Waddle, and here the trial took a dramatic turn. Bob Waddle had been born in Stoneham, Massachusetts, but grew up partly in Maine where his mother's family lived. After Malden High School he joined the U.S. Marines and served from 1948 to 1952, missing Korea because of an injury. Out of the military, he worked in a relative's gas station and dabbled in some college courses before heading for his mother's home at Cundy's Harbor, between Brunswick and Bailey Island, to be a fisherman and his own boss. In 1958 he was thirty years old, sported a crew cut, and had a youthful, firm, square-jawed look. He sat on the witness stand wearing a tweed jacket, starched khakis, and an open collar, composed and speaking clearly and looking Galgay straight in the eye. His wife, sitting in the spectator section, was scared. Bob Waddle, though, remembered hurrying to the grand jury room, anxious and uncertain, and talking too much to these federal hotshots. Now the ex-Marine and staunch believer in fishermen's rights would be anything but cooperative.

Waddle's reluctance to be forthcoming became immediately clear. Galgay, in fact, because of Waddle's studied vagueness and Grossman's objections, found it difficult merely to establish what Waddle did for a living. Eventually, Waddle described his work: "Well, I buy bait, salt bait, repair my boat, have a 31-foot cabin launch I fish out of, build traps, head traps, tend to gasoline and oil, I set traps; have a little over seven hundred traps, I haul over five hundred a day when I'm fishing. I fish six months out of the year." Waddle's gross income indicated that he was a "highliner": approximately $14,000, from which he figured he netted about $4,000. His overhead included $1,500 for gas, close to $3,000 for bait, more than $1,500 for rigging, trap maintenance, repair of wharf and fishhouse, etc., and 5 cents a pound on the lobster catch as pay for his sternman.

During 1957, Galgay determined, Waddle sold his lobsters to the Crawford Lobster Company of Kittery, Maine, which picked up lobsters twice a week at his pier. Galgay stressed that Waddle never refused the price that Crawford offered, while Waddle emphasized that "he tells me what he's paying" and "I can't refuse it and fish two days in a row." He never refused the price during 1957.

The going got especially sticky when Galgay turned to Waddle's MLA activities. He wanted to establish that after the July 19, 1957, meeting at the Harris Company in Portland, Waddle, as an MLA delegate, had returned to Cundy's Harbor and East Harpswell and agitated—as instructed by the MLA—to get fishermen in his area to tie up until dealers paid a better price.

Waddle could not remember, he said, what Les Dyer or anyone else had said. "Well, there were several people spoke at the meeting, but I couldn't connect any particular thing that was said with any person saying it." He conceded that price was discussed; but not until Galgay produced government exhibit no. 31 (the MLA's own summary of the meeting) did Waddle concur that a vote was taken to stop production in order to get a minimum price of 35 cents. Waddle refused to acknowledge that he carried an MLA message to Cundy's Harbor fishermen. To the contrary, it was just the men talking among themselves about what to do: "Nobody advised me" and "no instructions were given."

The government prosecutor soon lost patience and requested "that the witness might be declared hostile and allow the Government some latitude in inquiring along this line." Judge Gignoux knew of no provision in the *Criminal Rules* for such action, but Galgay countered that this could be allowed at the discretion of the court. In a brief conference at the bench, O'Donnell handed Gignoux a U.S. Attorney's Office manual containing a discussion of the point, but the judge was not yet satisfied that Waddle should be declared hostile.

Galgay then pursued Waddle's activities in spreading the word of the tie-up at East Harpswell, establishing that Waddle had phoned some fishermen but mostly had visited them on the water in his boat. "Well, I would run up alongside of them and say good morning and we would usually start discussing price anyway; that was the first thing a fisherman always talks about, and I would tell them that I wasn't going to haul today and the price had gone to 30 cents. Some of them would have a little bit of bait and they were going to use [it] up; some of them would turn around and go back in; some of them would haul if lobsters were 10 cents." Waddle had visited most of the fishermen from his area on the water, and believed he had asked only two of them "outright" to stop hauling. In any case, of the fifty fishermen at East Harpswell only three did not comply "with the vote that was taken on July 19, 1957." (The government wanted to show coercion, of course. Thirty-five years later, Robert Waddle recalled that there were only "a couple of old codgers" that he could not "talk in," but he remained friends with them.)

When the prosecution turned to the second tie-up, Grossman's objections and Waddle's steady evasions exasperated Galgay, who sharply reminded Waddle of a conference he had had with Galgay and Mr. Lewis about two weeks ago, when Waddle had been much more specific. Waddle retaliated by venting some of his resentment at Galgay: "When we had that conference, I was not on oath for one thing and for another thing, the only thing we were there for was to go over previous testimony and you said that the small talk didn't matter anyway. As I remember it, that was some of the small talk."

Further sparring led Galgay to renew his request that Waddle be declared a hostile witness, and Gignoux reluctantly did so (over Grossman's objection, of course). The judge gave Galgay permission to proceed with direct cross-examination. Soon after, the second day of the trial ended.

On Wednesday, May 21, at 9:30 A.M., the trial resumed with Judge Gignoux reminding the jury that Waddle was a hostile witness and with Galgay returning to the attack and Waddle to his shell of hazy recollection. Waddle said he went to the rooftop meeting at the Harris Company in Portland that past July because he wasn't doing anything else, knew neither the purpose nor the outcome of the meeting and, having stood in a doorway, could not hear very well. "Sort of a fruitless day for you, wasn't it," returned Galgay, sarcastically, "attending a meeting that you didn't hear Mr. Cushing say anything, you didn't hear Mr. Dyer say anything, you didn't know what the purpose of the meeting was and you don't know what transpired, is that your testimony?"

As Galgay turned next to the subject of cooperation by fishermen along the coast, Waddle shifted the focus to the consequences of the Down East men fishing during the first tie-up: "the dealers were still getting their lobsters and they . . . didn't care if the fishermen in this area rotted on the bank, they could get their lobsters, they didn't need us." Galgay, persisting: "At the time that the shedders first hit you, you needed the Downeast fishermen to tie up to make your strike effective, didn't you?" "It was not a strike, sir."

Galgay soon introduced an MLA document summarizing the August 7, 1957, Rockland meeting. He stressed two key passages: (1) "It was brought out . . . that 99 per cent of the lobstering had ceased in the second work stoppage in behalf of demands for at least 35 cents a pound from dealers"; (2) "[The meeting] voted on a motion to return to fishing under protest and continue talks with dealers; it was defeated in a secret ballot which newsmen present were drafted to count, 250 to 94."

Even Gignoux lost patience when Waddle said he *thought* that the Mr. Grossman referred to in the document was the same one in the courtroom. Finally, a dyspeptic Galgay yielded the witness to Grossman for cross-examination.

The defense attorney then emphasized, through questioning, that after the vote of the MLA *not* to fish, the fishermen of East Harpswell had nevertheless returned immediately to fishing. He repeated Waddle's phrase for the dealers' alleged insensitivity: "Your dealers here didn't care if you rotted on the banks." Grossman also revisited Waddle's lack of leverage in negotiating the daily boat-price: "You said that 'I can't refuse what he offers me.' " Waddle: "I said I couldn't refuse two days in a row. . . . We keep our lobsters in hundred-pound cars and we only have so many of them. You can't keep them [lobsters] in your cellar."

Grossman also offered as the first defense exhibit a red MLA banner. Galgay had stressed that Waddle had been flying an MLA flag from his mast when he visited fishermen on the water, and Grossman probably wanted to demystify the banner for the jury—it was not, after all, the Jolly Roger.

Mostly, Grossman concentrated (to objections from Galgay) on dealers' price-fixing, and he also kept asking if Waddle knew that "the dealers refused to discuss the matter of price [with the MLA] . . . during the summer of 1957." By the time Galgay succeeded in having Waddle's answer stricken from the record, Grossman had asked the question in different ways at least seven times.

Grossman, of course, was pursuing whenever he could precisely the line of defense that the judge had disallowed: namely, the response of the MLA to the dealers' price-fixing. Galgay and O'Donnell referred Gignoux to the *United States* v. *Socony Vacuum Oil Co.* case, heard by the Supreme Court, which established that the purpose of a price-fixing agreement and conspiracy is immaterial to a charge of violating the Sherman Act. For the time being, though, the judge granted Grossman leeway to stress his point that the MLA had sought arbitration while the dealers had not. The Rockland attorney, along with his colleague Stanley Tupper as personal counsel for Leslie Dyer, concluded with Waddle's concurrence that all MLA members "were free and independent businessmen and could conduct their business as they choose," and that the votes taken at MLA meetings in 1957 "were only opinion polls."

In redirect examination Galgay rose to taunt Waddle for the sudden improvement in his memory when answering Grossman's questions. He asked Waddle about the cooperative he and five other fishermen had formed after the tie-ups in order to market their lobsters, and he also elicited the surprising fact that throughout the tie-ups Waddle was receiving a price of 35 cents a pound for lobsters from his dealer, even though other fishermen were getting 30 cents. Galgay himself made the point—which might have enhanced Waddle's integrity in the eyes of the jury—that "you were out tying up your enterprise for a cause that didn't affect you at all." That phrasing of Galgay's, of course, ignored Waddle's commitment to a common good. Waddle's MLA loyalism, in fact, prompted him to make an admission that pleased Galgay: namely, that he had tied up because of the MLA. Despite a Grossman objection,

Waddle answered: "Yes. It had to do with that vote." This led to a furious struggle between Galgay and Grossman, with Waddle tugged back and forth between the two.

Grossman elicited from Waddle that when he went back fishing, it was "something that you did on your own," after which Galgay again wrung from a now weary Waddle the admission that his decision not to fish "wasn't made by you back in East Harpswell all by yourself?" "No, sir."

Grossman: "You were not obliged to follow any vote of the Association, were you?" "No, sir." And, over objections, Grossman repeated that the vote was an "opinion poll."

Galgay came back to ask Waddle if, at either the July 19 or the August 7 MLA meeting, he heard discussed "the words 'opinion polls.'" No, said Waddle. "Was the first time you heard that term applied to these meetings here today, when Mr. Grossman asked you that question?" "Yes, sir." Grossman again: "Isn't it a fact that when any votes were taken, they were termed 'polls'?" "Yes, sir." Finally, both lawyers signaled that they had no further questions. "THE COURT: Are all counsel satisfied? MR. GALGAY: I'm not satisfied, but I'm through. MR. GROSSMAN: I'm not satisfied, either, your Honor, but I'm through." So Robert Waddle left the stand.

The next fisherman called as a government witness proved no less evasive than Waddle, but he parried his interrogators with quick verbal footwork. Myles L. "Mike" O'Reilly Jr. was a classic Maine "character," full of himself and Irish blarney. The Irish, it is said, learned long ago how to fend off prying authority by using much talk to say nothing. Mike O'Reilly's wordplay left the government lawyers shaking their heads in frustration.

O'Reilly lived on Casco Bay's outermost Cliff Island, and in 1958 he was a thirty-five-year-old father of five. A small man, lean and windburned, with blue eyes and a round, bony face adorned with thin-rimmed round spectacles that gave him an owlish look (and the additional nickname "Doorknob"), O'Reilly's staccato answers to prosecution questions often brought hoots of laughter from the fishermen out front—as well as frowns (and suppressed smiles) from the judge.

Galgay, having dealt with O'Reilly during the grand jury inquiry, passed on this confounding fisherman to one of his junior colleagues: young, square Joe Nowlin.

Opening questions went smoothly enough. O'Reilly did a little mackerel fishing, but 99 percent of his business was lobstering. He normally ran four or five hundred traps and made a gross income the year before of between $8,000 and $9,000. He was not only a member of the MLA but had been elected the Cliff Island delegate. Here things slowed down. "At what time did you become a delegate?" "Well, I don't remember dates." "Do you remember what month it was?" "No I do not." "Was it in winter?" "Well, we had two winters in that year." "Well, was it in January or February?" No. "Was it in the spring?" "It could have been." "Was it in the summer?" Yes. Three questions and one objection later: "To tell you the truth, I don't know when it was, but some time during the summer I became a delegate."

Was it at a meeting of Cliff Island fishermen? No. Where then? "It was a meeting at the fire station, volunteer firemen." "Are the volunteer firemen the same people as the fishermen?" "They are; some of them." "So then it was at a firemen's meeting that you were elected as a delegate, is that correct?" "[O'Reilly smiling broadly] That's correct."

A few moments later, Nowlin asked O'Reilly how long he had been a member of the MLA. "Since the beginning of it." "When did it begin?" "I don't know." "Is it 10 years old, 20 years old, two years old?" "I wouldn't say it was 20, no." "You have been a member since its inception, you said?" "That's right." "Is it three years old?" "Could be." Here Nowlin fumed and said sharply: "Mr. O'Reilly, I wish you would answer, if you know, about how many years the organization has been in existence; if you don't know, of course, you can't answer, but if you do recall, how long have you been a member of the Association?" All innocence, O'Reilly patiently replied, "I told you, I didn't know." "Is it less than 10 years?" Yes. "Is it more than one year?" Yes. "How about three years?" "I don't know." Nowlin changed the subject. But in doing so, he got into deeper water, specifically the waters of nearby Casco Bay.

Nowlin was asking O'Reilly about an incident at the annual MLA convention in Rockland, and O'Reilly began: "Well, we, after the meeting was over, we got discussing our problems, and some of the boys from East—" "What do you mean by the 'East'?" A look of disbelief spread over O'Reilly's face. Then he owlishly peered over his glasses and slowly answered, "The East," as fishermen squirmed in their chairs, coughed, and otherwise muffled guffaws. Poor Nowlin kept on: "What area, what area specifically do you refer to?" Now, patiently, as if talking to a child, O'Reilly explained, "Well, anything east of Cliff Island." "Anything east of—" "Yes, down East." "But Cliff Island itself is not Down East?" O'Reilly quipped, "It isn't east of me," at which point Judge Gignoux quickly spun in his chair and hid his face, apparently to blow his nose, while the fishermen out front howled.

Nowlin eventually employed the same tactic that Galgay had used with Waddle, introducing the MLA's own reports of its meetings in 1957 which clearly discussed price and asking O'Reilly if these refreshed his memory. O'Reilly still managed to perplex Nowlin, and even claimed he could not recall "the 35 cent price" being discussed at the July 19 meeting. "Perhaps I misunderstood you. Do you recall a different version [of the document] or do you just have no recollection as to the matter, which is it, if either?" "I have no recollection of the matter." "Have you any recollection that is not consistent with what is reported in exhibit 31?" "You will have to speak plainer than that." "Well, maybe I will rephrase it." And so it went.

Asked about the report he gave back home after the July 19 MLA meeting, O'Reilly answered: "I didn't have much of a job to report what I had to tell. I come from a little place out here in the bay and everybody is 100 per cent Association, so you know how they felt and how I felt." O'Reilly represented about twenty-five fishermen on Cliff Island and took pride in their unity. Asked if all the fishermen on the island had tied up in July, he shot back, "Every damn one of them," earning a request from the judge to "refrain from profanity in the courtroom." Regarding whether the island fishermen held a meeting on whether to tie up, he said: "At Cliff Island we don't have to have a meeting. The place is small. We have a grocery store and we congregate in the grocery store." Later, when Nowlin asked if the Cliff Islanders had held a meeting before the second tie-up: "We had very few meetings at Cliff Island." A resigned Nowlin: "It isn't necessary, I take it?" "No. You can tell the President of the Mothers' Club or something like that."

O'Reilly clearly had watched closely during the questioning of

Waddle and learned from it above all to throttle his memory and take refuge in Delphic ambiguity. Soon after Grossman had objected to an overly long question of Nowlin's as containing two or three questions, O'Reilly—a quick study—greeted another long Nowlin question with, "You have two questions before you give me a chance to answer one." What he could and could not remember defied all logic.

Nowlin savored a brief moment of revenge, however, when he queried O'Reilly about what specifically he had said at the MLA meeting about the second tie-up. Though he knew the question was leading, Nowlin asked if O'Reilly recalled "saying at the Rockland meeting that the Cliff Island fishermen were 100 per cent willing to stay ashore 'till hell froze over and they would have, too, period?" Judge Gignoux immediately directed O'Reilly not to answer the question and sustained Grossman's objection. Then Nowlin finished and Grossman began cross-examination.

Coached by Grossman's questions, O'Reilly recalled that at the Harris rooftop meeting he had gotten up on "the bucket" or "soap box" and suggested that "the boys tie up" because he thought "it would be discourteous" to Governor Muskie not to wait until they could find out what he might do for them. Grossman also returned to O'Reilly's astonishing but stubborn claim that he did not recall a 35 cent price being discussed at the July 19 meeting. Regarding whether he discussed the matter with Les Dyer, O'Reilly provoked another judicial reprimand when he declared, "I didn't know that that [mention of the 35 cent price] was on that paper until I was brainwashed downstairs." Grossman returned, too, to his mantra that any MLA votes were "merely polls" and that "each and every member could go home and fish or not fish." Did O'Reilly have anything to say as to how much he should get for his lobsters? "Well, the way the question is worded—I have plenty to say but it doesn't do me any good."

But Nowlin wanted the last spin on the matter of what he saw as O'Reilly's freedom to sell to whomever he wished. "Is there anything to compel you to take the price offered by any particular dealer?" Yes. "What is that?" "Well, I have to feed my children. I have to sell my lobsters." "Does that consideration influence you to deal with one dealer rather than another?" "They're all alike." Told by Gignoux to answer the question, his last words were "No, sir."

The lawyers on both sides had no further questions for O'Reilly, but he was not quite finished with *them*. During the next recess, O'Reilly approached a startled Nowlin and Galgay out in the corridor, and tried to engage them in conversation. Persuaded finally that under court rules this could not be done, O'Reilly turned away, but not before impishly hurling over his shoulder, "If you'd asked me the right questions, I'd a-told you more."

The next government witness proved to be much less of a problem for Alan Lewis, who again took the baton for the government in his matter-of-fact style. Fifty-four-year-old Elmer C. Alley cut a neat, compact figure at five feet five inches and 130–40 pounds. He had salt-and-pepper brown hair and blue eyes, and was known in his Down East town of Prospect Harbor as a kindly, religious man, helpful to his neighbors and fellow fishermen. His father had been a lobsterman, trawler, and sardine fisher, and Elmer had fished for lobsters for thirty-four years. Serving in the Coast Guard at Isle of Shoals during the war, Alley like many others had bought a larger powerboat during the postwar boom in the lobster fishery. He proudly described his "34-foot cabin boat with a 9-foot beam, with a large Buick motor, nine years old this month." Alley, as was more common Down East, fished far fewer traps than a Bob Waddle, 125 to 150; his gross income was only $5,000, and he estimated his net to be about half that figure. Sober, courteous, and direct in his manner, Alley would try to avoid saying things damaging to Leslie Dyer or the MLA—which he fervently believed in—but his unaffected sincerity made him vulnerable to Lewis's probing.

Yet at the start of his interrogation of Alley, Lewis, like Nowlin, stumbled over another peculiarity of the coast when he simply asked Alley where he lobstered. "Well, for the last two or three years, I fish between Scoodic Island and 'Tit Manan." Lewis's eyebrows arched, he gave an embarrassed cough, and giggles ran through the audience of fishermen and their wives. "Could you spell that for us, Mr. Alley?" "You mean Scoodic Island?" "Both of them, if you will, please." Puzzled, and misunderstanding, Alley obliged. "Well, I guess it's S-c-o-o-d-i-c." "And the second word?" (Irene Arabian, the stenographer, worked hard to stifle a smile as she waited patiently for the spelling.) Puzzled again, Alley simply said "Island." Lewis: "No—" Alley, helpfully: "'Tit Manan?" "Yes." "P-e-t-i-t-m-a-n-a-n I believe [Relief on Lewis's face]. If that's not right, you'll find it on the chart." More giggles.

After establishing that Alley was an MLA delegate who represented some twenty fishermen at Prospect Harbor, Lewis suspended his examination as court recessed for the day.

Thursday, May 22, 1958. The trial resumed on a typical early-spring day, partly sunny, with the temperature in Portland reaching a cool but mild sixty-five degrees. At 9:30 A.M. Alan Lewis breezed into his questioning of Elmer Alley. Alley agreed that at the July 19 MLA meeting Les Dyer had told the assembled fishermen that "we couldn't fish for 30 cents," that the dealers intended to drop to 25 cents, and "he figured we could fish on a 35 cent basis" and still make money. Alley testified further that he himself had risen to say that he could not fish for 30 cents and "was willing to tie up until a price was established that we could . . . make a dollar for ourselves."

The government had called this small producer from Down East to the trial mainly because they had in hand a letter that Alley had written to Leslie Dyer on August 6, 1957:

> Dear President,
>
> Just a few lines this morning to let you know how things are going down here.
>
> We have a very few old faithfuls that are still in but one or two have kept at it until they have pulled out all of South Gouldsboro. Winter [Harbor] went yesterday. I am sending you a clipping from the Maine Coast fishermen [sic] of the ring leader of Corea. He has caused the trouble over there and he draws a good Government pension. . . .
>
> I do hope things will be straightened out before the rest of the group gives in.
>
> The lobster truck was in Corea and got the lobsters from the three buyers there, so that is not too good.
>
> The fishermen are about all down here talking of a Coast wise

*close[d] season. . . . Many are in favor [of] handling their own
lobsters as a corporation.*

    *No matter what happens now we will try and keep our Associa-
tion. I know some have said that they would pay perhaps ten dollars if need be to keep it going so the dealers wouldn't bust us up.*

    *One thing that has hurt down this way is the one or two leaders
but another is that we haven't earned anything. . . . If such a thing
should happen again we should know how many were going to
tie-up and all do it together, but I don't think we could tie up
again this fall. Guess they will have to take what they get, and if
we don't get thirty five cents they may learn their lesson.*

    Trust things will turn out for the best . . .

      With best wishes,

        Elmer

  *P.S. Francis does not belong to the Assoc. and won't join. One of
my best members was over there to Corea yesterday and Francis's
father said I would like to see them tow Wilt [his son] in. His
father buys lobsters. . . .*

    The government regarded this letter as clear evidence of coercion
against noncooperating fishermen. Alley admitted to talking to several
men on the telephone and asking them to stay in, but that was the
extent of it. No one even threatened to tow in Wilson "Wilt" Francis,
referred to in the letter. But Alley, the MLA loyalist ("I was the last one
that left the mooring" when the tie-up ended), had given the prosecu-
tors their best haul of testimony so far. Grossman and Tupper declined
to question him.

    Another Down East lobsterman took the witness stand. "Rolling-
gaited" and wearing a maroon sweater, Irving Eugene Bracy of Port
Clyde was about forty years old, five feet ten inches, 180–90 pounds,
with thinning dark-brown hair and brown eyes behind wire-rimmed
spectacles. He had been lobsterfishing since shortly after the war and
was now the proud owner of "a 30-foot boat built Downeast, Stoning-
ton. It's 8 foot, 10 inches wide . . . and has a cabin and standing top with
a Chevrolet engine and a Paragon reverse gear and a Bendix recorder

and a Philco radio-telephone." At the height of the season, he fished about two hundred fifty traps.

John Galgay questioned Bracy and soon found him to be a master of circuitous talk. The government had called Bracy to show MLA coercion, but Galgay did not get very far. He did learn that Bracy represented about twenty-five Port Clyde fishermen to the MLA, and that he had resigned as a delegate during 1957 because he believed the tie-ups had been ended too quickly. Soon Galgay was sarcastically addressing Bracy as "Mr. Witness." After the judge sustained yet another of Grossman's objections and reminded Galgay that "this is still your witness," Galgay sputtered: "Not a very good one."

What did Bracy do in Port Clyde after the July 19 MLA meeting? "Well, I guess I fell into the customary routine. I think I had supper and, well, reported back, so to speak; in other words, I just went home. I don't remember that I did anything special." Galgay pressed on. With whom did Bracy talk about the MLA meeting? "Oh, well, different fellows that I met in my travels; sometimes it might take me a half an hour to get home . . . from over town." Galgay: Were they fishermen? Did Bracy talk with members as well as nonmembers of the MLA? "I talked with anybody who was willing to talk to me. I love to talk."

How did he describe to them the July 19 Rockland meeting? "I told them that the crowd as a whole wanted to tie the boats up, were planning to tie the boats up and holding turns so to speak for a while." At hearing the expression "holding turns" Galgay's eyes widened, and he rose on the balls of his feet. This sounded like the MLA men were taking turns patrolling the water to chase in noncompliers. "*Holding turns?*" he asked weightily. "Yes, sir," said Bracy, cheerfully. "What does that mean?" Bracy: "Well, I suppose that comes from the fact that when you are using a winch to hoist a load, that by taking extra turns on it you can hoist it up and if you hold a turn by letting the winch turn and you—" By now the judge was holding his hand over a smile, and soft, knowing laughter was rippling through the room. Galgay quickly recovered himself: "What it means is to stop them?" Bracy: "That, so to speak Down East is holding turn; in other words, stopping." Galgay, graciously conceding defeat and managing a small smile: "Thank you very much." Bracy, smiling back: "You're welcome, Mr. Galgay."

In cross-examination Grossman revealed that Bracy, several weeks before the trial began, had prompted a spirited encounter between himself and government lawyers Bloom and Nowlin. It seems that Galgay had called Bracy and asked him to meet the two attorneys in Rockland at the Thorndike Hotel. Bracy came to the lobby but was accompanied by Grossman, and said he would answer any question put to him—but only in Grossman's presence. "Quite a heated discussion took place in the lobby between the Government attorneys and myself?" Bracy, with classic fishermen's understatement: "Yes, it was a little bit warm."

Bracy also responded crisply to Stanley Tupper's emphasis again, in a further attempt to build a defense for Leslie Dyer, that lobstermen fish whenever they want to regardless of what anyone suggests. "Yes, I guess I am kind of bull-headed. . . . I never felt at any time that I wasn't a free agent."

Galgay got Bracy to concede that at the Thorndike meeting the government lawyers had told him that he was under no obligation to talk to them. But Bracy at the last slipped off Galgay's hook. Confronted with Galgay's quotation from the MLA's August 7 meeting that lobstering had ceased "in behalf of demands for at least 35 cents," Bracy owned to having voted "to keep my boat on the mooring," but claimed—assisted by Grossman's objections—"I can't remember for sure that any specific price was discussed."

Alger Burgess would take the stand next, as the first week of the trial was drawing to a close. Like Bob Waddle and other MLA loyalists, he took a broad view of the lobster industry and was easily the most combative witness the government lawyers confronted. Burgess's testimony would push the trial to a new, higher level of tension.

Wearing a tweed jacket and freshly pressed flannel pants, Alger Burgess took the stand and in a relaxed manner gave the details of his work as a fisherman to Alan Lewis. Alger had been a "lobstercatcher" for twenty years, and ran about three hundred traps at the height of the season. He was one of forty-five or so fishermen on Chebeague Island, about half of whom were MLA members, and one of two island delegates. While in the Coast Guard during the war, an automobile accident had damaged his hearing. Alger often spoke too softly; and frequently, of course, he could not hear Lewis, or chose not to hear. At the bench, Alan Grossman defended the witness to the judge and to Lewis as impaired by a "war injury" and not unresponsive, but Alger's defiance was often transparent.

His recollection regarding the MLA and lobster prices seemed non-existent, though he mentioned as often as he could the high cost of bait. When asked almost condescendingly if he understood a particular question, Burgess responded evenly: "I think I understood you pretty well. I don't think I could tell you one cussed word that anybody said that day." Pressed further on the July 1957 MLA meeting as to who spoke at it: "Oh, gorry, I wouldn't have any idea who the people was. They was all strangers to me."

Lewis: "I say when did you speak to these lobster fishermen about their hauling their traps?" "You asked me when did I speak to them?" Yes. "I don't know who you're referring to, so I can't answer the question." Lewis had the next-to-the-last question read back to the witness, then continued: "Now, you say 'not during that time.' My next question is when did you speak to them?" "You don't make yourself clear enough so I understand what you mean."

But Alger Burgess knew very well what Lewis was after when he asked him about a fellow lobsterman from his island, Ray Hamilton. Alger had gone out in his boat with several other MLA members during the tie-up and visited Hamilton, who had attended a local meeting at which the men agreed to tie up. Hamilton had told us he would go along with us, said Burgess, and we asked him "just why he was breaking his word to the men." What did Mr. Hamilton say to you? Burgess declined to "bring it up because it's pretty embarrassing."

At a bench conference, Lewis now made two requests: that the witness answer, self-censoring any profanity; and that Burgess be declared a hostile witness. The judge agreed to the excision of "colorful language" but reserved his decision on the second part.

Resuming, Burgess recalled that Hamilton had been asked about the price of lobsters "and he said he didn't give a you-know-what-I-mean about the price of lobsters. He said he could afford to go for nothing, he liked to do it because it was a lot of fun." After more such talk "we kind of laughed at him, and it made him pretty mad"; and he finally said he'd accomplished his purpose and was going in," and we had it understood with him that he was not forced to go ashore" and just wanted to know why he was hauling his traps when he said he wouldn't. "Well, then he told us about his wife, she was so ugly; that was the reason he was off hauling his traps, because he has no other choice." After that, said Burgess, they felt sorry for a man so bullied by his wife, so they left him be.

Lewis asked next about Burgess's encounter with another fisherman out on the water during the tie-up, Clayton Johnson of Bailey's Island. Johnson "said they didn't agree with us down there, they was all hauling traps, and I asked him why . . . and he says, 'I'm getting my price, I can afford to go for my price.' "

Soon after, Lewis approached the bench and again asked that Burgess be declared a hostile witness. Gignoux: "The Court has observed this witness roughly for two hours . . . and has concluded that he appears to be distinctly evasive . . . reluctant to respond to questions which are put to him by the Government." Request granted.

But this did not help Lewis much. Burgess refused to acknowledge the 35 cent price, would say only that 30 cents was too low, and even claimed that he was holding out for 37 cents. He also denied that he ever heard Ray Hamilton say, "You fellas can cut away my gear, you can do anything but I'm still going to haul my traps." Reprimanded for profanity ("hell") and for arguing with counsel, Burgess remained a difficult witness.

Toward the end of the day, though, after a long stint on the stand, he tired. Asked if he went out in his boat during the tie-up "and patrolled around the Chebeague Island area" to speak to any men out fishing, Burgess answered: "I wouldn't say that, no." But then: "How many people did you speak to while you were patrolling around, if you spoke to any?" "It would be hard to say. There was quite a number." He guessed eight or ten, and "they was very gentlemanly and most of them went home . . . and some of them just laughed at us and threw us a bottle of beer and they kept right on hauling their traps, and that was the last we said to them." The prosecution had wanted very much to establish the term "patrolling," and Alger Burgess finally gave in to it.

One brief exchange between Lewis and Burgess showed the gulf between the lawyer and the fisherman. "If you all tied up at the same time [at Chebeague Island], did you speak to them at the time you tied up?"

Burgess, with a fisherman's understatement: "That would have been quite a job." Lewis, oblivious: "Well, was it just a particular day arrived and everybody just didn't go?" The island is relatively small, perhaps four miles by two at its longest and widest, but with an irregular shore. Like the rest of the Maine coast, there are numerous coves which have served as mooring places, perhaps a dozen or more. To talk to men as they tied up at each of these would have been, indeed, "quite a job."

4 WEEK TWO

"I haven't broke no law of any kind."
—*Alger Burgess*

he second week of the trial opened not with Alger Burgess on the stand but instead with the government questioning a tall, slender, handsome young man in his twenties from Port Clyde. Robert J. Davis was no longer a fisherman—he now lived in Florida and was first mate on a missile recovery boat stationed at Fort Canaveral. Indeed, Davis had been something of a "summer dubber," having grown up in the Rockland-Thomaston area and coming from a family that owned a funeral home. With reddish-blond hair and a thin mustache, Davis had been known for hell-raising as a teenager and as something of a ladies' man. Part of his "wild youth"—by Maine standards—included spending several summers living in a fish house on Monhegan Island "to do his own thing." In the summer of 1957, however, Davis owned a powerboat, fished three hundred traps, and earned a gross income of $3,500. He had also been appointed temporarily as an MLA delegate and had helped Irving Bracy and others organize meetings among Port Clyde and Tenant's Harbor fishermen.

Questioned by John Galgay, the smooth-talking Davis, who had attended a private academy briefly before being suspended, contested even the terms Galgay used to describe his actions. Thus, Davis said, he returned home after the Rockland MLA meeting "under the impression that I should be somewhat of a missionary" to explain how things were along the coast. Galgay: "Did you tell us anything else that took place with regard to the instructions other than [your] acting as missionary?" "I believe you misunderstood me. I never had any instructions." Later on, Galgay again used the word "instructions" and Davis retorted: "I don't believe Mr. Bracy gave anybody instructions. I don't believe you could give any lobster fisherman any instructions."

Davis echoed Grossman in labeling all MLA votes as "opinion polls." He did not do any "patrolling" of the waters during the tie-ups, but he did visit fishermen out on the water. He even challenged Galgay, implicitly, every time he asked a question about Dyer or Bracy *presiding* over or *conducting* a meeting, substituting instead the word "moderator."

But it was Davis's almost total lack of recall regarding votes for a 35 cent price that irritated Galgay and soon had him calling Davis "Mr. Witness." Indeed, Galgay took far less time than he had with Waddle or Burgess to ask the court to declare Davis a hostile witness. Gignoux quickly declared that he was "fully conscious that this witness is a lobster fisherman and a member of the Maine Lobstermen's Association [neither of which was true at the moment] and is most certainly hostile to the Government counsel."

His new status made Davis no more forthcoming. This led Galgay to read from the transcript of Davis's grand jury testimony, a move that concerned the judge and that Grossman had warned would prompt him to request the same material. But when Galgay quoted Davis saying that Bracy has urged everyone to support the MLA resolve to tie up for a 35 cents, the best that Galgay received in response was: "Gorry, I don't recall saying that, but if you have got it there, I must have." Galgay kept pressing: "Are you saying he didn't say that?" "No, I can't say that he didn't either. If I can't recall it one way or the other, I can't say he did and I can't say he didn't." Despite a barrage of questions from Galgay, Davis tenaciously stayed with this line. Galgay, however, read several excerpts from Davis's grand jury testimony, all damaging to the defense.

When Grossman was offered the opportunity to cross-examine, he instead requested a copy of the grand jury testimony to read before proceeding. At this point, the morning session ended and counsel met with the judge in chambers to discuss Grossman's request. There Grossman argued that the government itself had removed the "cloak of secrecy" from the testimony and that simple fairness demanded the defense be given the same privilege. Nowlin defended the government's limited use of the testimony and denied that the defense possessed any rights to it. He again cited the government's standard of *Socony Vacuum Oil.* Yet Nowlin himself suggested a way out by referring to a recent New York case, *Consolidated Laundries Corporation,* in which a judge had granted to the defense access to grand jury testimony—limited to those parts relevant to what had already been disclosed—following the judge's examination and at his discretion. Gignoux reminded Nowlin of his earlier warning, and decided to review Davis's previous testimony and then let the defense see selected pages. After lunch and a brief conference confirming the agreement, the trial resumed at 1:30 P.M. with Alger Burgess back on the stand.

Alan Lewis immediately confronted Burgess with his answers from the grand jury testimony given several months before. He focused on the MLA vote for a 35 cent price, on Burgess's encounter with Ray Hamilton, and on his extensive "patrolling" during the tie-ups. But the Chebeague Island fisherman, while assenting that he recalled testifying according to the record, generally would not say that that was his recollection *now.* Lewis: "Did the record that I have just read to you refresh your recollection at all?" "Not a bit." "As to what Mr. Dyer said?" "Not a bit." "You do recall having testified as I have just indicated before the grand jury?" "That's right." In general, said Burgess, "If that is what I said to the grand jury that is just as sure as can be probably what I said. I don't wish to lie to anybody. . . . I was under oath just the same as I am now, but if you ask me to remember that [now], I couldn't remember that for five seconds." When it came, however, to having claimed that he "did more patrolling as a delegate along the coast of

Maine than any other delegate," Burgess's pride may have prevailed, and he agreed that he probably did.

Alan Grossman used his cross-examination to try to create sympathy for Alger Burgess and for his clients. Burgess was a partially disabled veteran of World War II, Grossman stressed, making the most of Alger's damaged hearing. He had been ganged up on at the grand jury hearing, Grossman implied, by three or four government lawyers. Asked if he were at ease then, Burgess answered no, "I [was] just like I am right now. I was scared right to death." His gross income, which Grossman sarcastically mentioned the government had neglected to disclose, was no more than $5,000, and the net income of this economic malefactor was just under $3,000. With the dealers raising the price of bait and imposing a 30 cent price, said Grossman, "whether or not there was an association . . . the men at Chebeague Island couldn't afford to fish and wouldn't have fished anyway for that price."

This line of questioning climaxed when Grossman asked Burgess if it were true that Mr. Dyer never told him or anyone else in his presence that they had to do anything. Burgess asked if he could answer that "the way I want to." Certainly. He began by saying in a low voice that he did not expect any special privileges as a veteran, then continued in a stronger voice, with emotion: "But the thing of it is I feel that we are still living in the United States and I don't have to have anybody tell me what I can do, not Leslie Dyer or these men here or you or anybody else, unless I am breaking the law and then I expect it, but as I see it, I haven't broke no law of any kind, and I don't have to have anybody tell me what to do. I still hope that I am a free man."

In redirect examination, Alan Lewis sought to deflate the effect of this by challenging Burgess's statement that Portland dealers refused to buy lobsters from him. Burgess, said Lewis, *was* a free agent because he had not gone to every single Portland dealer seeking a better price. Lewis wanted also to dispel the impression that Burgess had somehow been "abused" at the grand jury hearing. Burgess: "I wouldn't say abused, no. I would say that I was just pretty ignorant what was going on." Were his rights explained? "Only that . . . Mr. Galgay himself told me that what I told him there, that day, would never ever be mentioned again to nobody except just between me and him and the grand jury."

"Wasn't there a friendly atmosphere?" "Oh, I don't know what you call 'friendly'?" Asked how long he had been there, he said: "It seems to me that I was in there for a week." "You were not abused, correct?" "Oh, I don't think they beat me over the head with a hose or anything of the kind." "But you did answer questions there truthfully?" Yes. At that Lewis concluded. Grossman, who had requested the pages from Burgess's grand jury testimony, now withdrew that request out of consideration for Burgess, and so Alger Burgess was finally excused.

Robert Davis returned to the stand briefly. He was addressed crisply by Galgay, who again asked questions framed by Davis's grand jury testimony. The best he got from Davis, however, was no more than, "I imagine I did."

The last witness that day was another Chebeague Island fisherman, Albion Miller, who had served as an MLA delegate with Alger Burgess during 1957 but was no longer an association member. Alan Lewis pursued—though not extensively—issues similar to those raised with Burgess. But if witnesses such as Burgess, Davis, and Waddle had made a mixed impression on the jury, Albion Miller now cast the alleged criminal conspirators in a sympathetic glow.

Fifty-seven years old in 1958, Albion Miller had been a fisherman of one sort or another all his life. Now he fished from a cove in front of his small house on Chebeague where all summer long he climbed up and down a steep bank to his outboard-powered dory. These exertions made him slightly stooped, though he still stood well over six feet tall. He was a simple, charming man, consistently cheerful and humorous, with receding blond-white hair and an open face with friendly blue eyes. He spoke with a rounded twang and kindly manner that made him sound like one of Santa's helpers. The fishermen all liked and trusted Albion. Everyone did.

Little of Albion's humor came through in his testimony, but—unhampered by any testimony to the grand jury at a time when he might have been taken unawares—he succeeded in parrying every thrust by Lewis. He recalled going to two MLA meetings in Rockland and calling a meeting on Chebeague, yet not much else. Everyone agreed that prices were too low (he had been getting 32 cents), but no one price was agreed upon for going back to work. Les Dyer called the meetings to order. Albion recalled none of the palaver around the hall.

He remembered no votes. Government exhibits failed to refresh his memory. "What was the general opinion among the group as to what was a fair return?" "Well, the most general opinion, that we had to get enough to keep the wolf from the door." "Well, what was that price that would keep the wolf from the door?" "There was no specific price."

Miller guessed that his gross income from lobstering was "around twenty-two or twenty-three hundred dollars." "That was the gross?" a somewhat disbelieving Lewis asked. "Of that," he continued, insensitively, "what was your net?" "Well, I think around fifteen to sixteen hundred dollars on my lobsters. Of course, I go fishing part time." And the gross value of other sales? Here Grossman intervened: "I don't see what bearing that has here." Gignoux, understanding an older islander-fisherman's simple life-style, upheld the objection with a look to Lewis that instructed him to leave it alone.

Having scored heavily with Burgess and Davis, the government washed out with Albion Miller. The defense had no questions for him, but he had helped them merely by his presence. Miller left the stand, and the court adjourned for the day at 3:55 P.M.

At 4 P.M., however, counsel met with Gignoux in chambers to debate again the government's reading from grand jury minutes. The government lawyers now took the offensive on this issue, calling Gignoux's attention to a 1925 case in which a circuit court had ruled that a jury might base its verdict on "prior statements of a witness before a Grand Jury and was not confined to . . . 'the truth of words uttered under oath in Court.'" But the judge had himself reviewed several cases and would not admit the earlier statements as substantive. He stuck with his earlier decision to grant the defense access to the minutes used by the prosecution.

Nowlin next asserted that Burgess and Davis in effect had validated the earlier testimony and so grandfathered it into the record. But Gignoux disagreed. As *he* recalled Burgess's testimony—"He seemed to say: 'Well, if you say I said it, I must have, or words to that effect.'" Nowlin then retreated and rephrased what the judge had said: "Some of them edged awfully close to it but they don't cross the line." Gignoux then promised to review the testimony carefully, and with this fifteen-minute conference the first day of the second week ended.

At 9:15 the next morning (Tuesday, May 27) the struggle resumed in the judge's chambers. It opened dramatically with the defense presenting a motion for a mistrial. John Knight appealed to the government's own template case, *United States* v. *Socony Vacuum Oil Co.,* for ammunition. There the Supreme Court had said that if previous testimony (such as the grand jury minutes) were used deliberately not for purposes relevant to the issues "but to arouse the passions of the jurors," or if, under the "pretext of refreshing a witness's recollection, the prior testimony was introduced as evidence," then there would be grounds for reversible error. Knight contended also that "much more than was needed" had been read and, while acknowledging the judge's warning to the jury, argued that as normal human beings the jury would nonetheless be affected by what they heard.

Nowlin replied that the material had been submitted in good faith and pointed out that all the information discussed was already in evidence by way of the MLA's own documents—and thus existed independently anyway. To this Alan Grossman retorted that the government had shown its intent the evening before when it claimed that the judge was in error and tried to get him to admit the prior testimony as full-fledged evidence—which Gignoux had rejected. The judge replied that the government had made that request in chambers and not before the jury, so he rejected Grossman's reasoning, stood by his previous rulings, and denied the motion for a mistrial. The defense emerged from the twenty-five-minute conference only with the advantage of having in its hands the minutes of Davis's grand jury testimony for Grossman's cross-examination.

Grossman again tried to generate sympathy for a young fisherman brought before a grand jury for the first time in his life. When Grossman read from the grand jury minutes, he did so to suggest again that this fisherman—like others—had been misled. Galgay had been asking Davis how many fishermen had attended a meeting and seeking an approximate number. Grossman quoted Galgay's question: "Well, just give us the best estimate you can. *You're not going to be persecuted or prosecuted if you miss.*" "Did you understand what he was saying to you?" Grossman asked Davis. "I don't know as I understood it, but I was under the impression that it would never go out of that room, anything that I said that day."

Following his earlier strategy, Grossman did his best to use Davis as a witness for the defense. But Galgay raised frequent objections, and at crucial points Judge Gignoux admonished Grossman to wait until the defense presented its own witnesses. Galgay used redirect examination mainly to taunt Davis for his splendidly improved memory when responding to Grossman. Davis was now excused, and the judge called a fifteen-minute recess.

Up to now the trial had possessed elements of drama and comedy as well as tiresome technicalities. With the next government witness, however, it entered the realm of melodrama and bathos. Judge Gignoux felt compelled to warn counsel at the bench that "we don't want to make this into a circus." But the Reverend John Taylor Holman, from Port Clyde, a minister, fisherman, and Maine original, already had attracted considerable publicity because of claims of persecution. He was to be the prosecution's star witness, and he relished the role as he tearfully told the jury of threats on his life and his divinely guided decision to stand by his principles and keep fishing. But the more he talked, and Alan Grossman encouraged him to do just that, the more tangled his testimony became.

Holman was a spry sixty-one-year-old, short and portly, with a broad grandfatherly face and receding white hair. He made a good first impression, wearing a neat blue suit, white shirt and dark tie, and speaking clearly and firmly, often with dramatic emphasis. He obviously enjoyed having the witness box as a forum. But even John Galgay realized that the garrulous Holman was something of a loose cannon. Not five minutes into the testimony Gignoux became impatient with the witness's speechifying, and sharply instructed him to answer only the questions asked by counsel: "This, sir, is a Court of law." "Your Honor, sir, I was trying . . ." "No further statement is indicated."

Holman said he had been a minister for forty-four years and a lobsterman for the past fifteen. He had not had a settled church for some twenty years, but as an "evangelistic" preacher held revivals and "union campaigns" everywhere among various Protestant denominations. He fished only 70 to 120 traps from a small, fourteen-foot dory, which he rowed, and in 1957 he made a gross income from lobstering of $2,300. Holman said he refused to stop fishing because, not having a powerboat, he would be unable to move out into deeper water later in the season; so he needed to catch his lobsters then.

But there were many other reasons. When Robert Davis had visited him at his home and asked him and his son to join the MLA, Holman had tearfully told Davis that he needed money to help support five grandchildren and to help his son begin college in the fall. Holman also told Davis that he could not go to fishermen's meetings because they all smoked and that made him sick. And there was more. "I said, 'Bobby, you know as well as I do that the lobster fishermen of the State of Maine have been the goats of a Reciprocal Trade Treaty . . . you know that the Government permitted three weeks extra fishing in Nova Scotia, in Canada; and because of those three weeks extra fishing, our market is glutted." Interspersed with anecdotes going back to 1921 and designed to show his rectitude, Holman returned to his theme that Maine's senators and representatives in Washington had never done anything for Maine fishermen, and that he had known them always to abide by the rule that "the Government of Canada, by Canada and for Canada shall not perish from the State of Maine."

Galgay, wide-eyed: "This was all in a conversation that you had with . . ." "Absolutely, in my home. . . . I'm not through with it." "Well, by all means continue." Continue he did, frequently striking the pose of loyal citizen: he could not work with the MLA because he "must stand for the laws of my Government." At one point Galgay, with exquisitely subtle humor, asked: "Now did Mr. Davis get a chance to say anything?" "Any time he wanted, he broke in." Grossman here objected to Galgay interrupting his own witness, and Holman continued, describing now a sick and apparently impoverished son-in-law with a family of nine children as well as his expenses incurred as a preacher responding to church calls. So it was impossible for him to quit lobstering, and though he did not recall what Davis said in reply, "My tears were rolling down my cheeks, and I think he saw the burden I had."

Next Holman described for Galgay being visited on the water two separate times by Port Clyde fishermen who asked him to come in, and he now asked for chalk and blackboard to make a rough map of the shoreline and islands to locate the incidents. When the judge asked Grossman if he had any objection, he wryly replied: "May I say to the

Court that anything that might assist this witness, we have no objections at all."

On August 6, 1957, at the eastern end of Hart's Island, Robert Davis and two other fishermen in a boat hailed both Holman and his son John and asked them to come in. Holman refused. Davis was "a perfect gentleman," but Leroy Cushman broke in and asked Holman what kind of minister he was and if he didn't believe in the Golden Rule and so on. Then came a threat: "If you don't come in, you won't have a thing left in the ocean." At this point in his testimony, Holman broke down and cried a bit as he described his son John's reply (for which he claimed he reprimanded him afterward). If they touched his gear, "I have a .30-30 rifle, and there will not be one boat left afloat in Port Clyde Harbor."

The next day, Holman and his son were approached again, this time by a boat containing eight fishermen, including Davis. Holman rowed away into shallow water (where the bigger boat would not follow) because, he said, he feared for his life. But the men in the boat persuaded him to come closer to talk, and he did. They began by inviting him to come to a meeting, but his insistence on continuing to fish brought forth another chorus of recrimination. Holman in turn taunted them for not going after a couple of other fishermen who were ignoring the tie-up. They were afraid to pick on Laddie Myrick of Elliott, he said, because "if you dared go over there, he'd take a gun and shoot you, and you know it." They replied by throwing a loaf of bread in his boat, saying, "If you're hungry, we'll give you a loaf of bread." Then they threw pennies into his boat. Galgay produced "the very pennies." Galgay finished by having Holman tell of seeing two other fishermen being visited by the same group that had accosted him and then ceasing to haul traps.

Alan Grossman smiled as he approached the witness for cross-examination and began by establishing that he and Holman had known each other for fifteen years and occasionally held friendly chats on the streets of Rockland. But their exchanges quickly became adversarial as Grossman challenged Holman's credibility. His strategy was twofold: to display contradictions and to let Holman hang himself by his own excesses. Holman fought him every step, though, and often sidestepped the traps Grossman laid for him. But Holman also took the bait many times, especially when he could expound his "principles" and proclaim his integrity.

Holman had begun testifying at midmorning on Tuesday, May 27, and Grossman took up cross-examination shortly before noon. He kept Holman on the stand for the entire afternoon and part of the next morning in an effort to show Holman, as he put it to the judge at the bench, as "extremely hostile to the MLA" and in general "extremely prejudiced . . . [and] at least in the community that I live in . . . [he] is regarded as an odd individual, to put it mildly."

No sooner had Grossman begun than Holman took the offensive by introducing new evidence of his persecution: namely, that he had been shot at for fishing. Grossman questioned Holman about this incident repeatedly through the several hours of testimony, but he also peppered Holman on and off with questions about his manifold feuds with local courts, law enforcement officers, the public schools, the press, and other fishermen.

August 3, Holman said, was "when they fired the rifle at me," and he spent the next day resisting pleas from his son ("Daddy, they'll kill you") and his wife ("John, how can we live without you"). Kneeling beside his bed, however, he knew his principles were "God first, my Government second, my family third, my neighbors and friends fourth." As he rambled, Holman suddenly mentioned his inability to get results from the Knox County courts regarding his son, "and you haven't even declared him innocent yet, and that's eighteen months ago; and I've asked you, Judge, and asked you, Judge, over and over again to get it." Here Judge Gignoux (who was not the judge in question) intervened, and shortly thereafter the noon recess came.

After lunch Holman revealed that his son had been fined for driving 60 mph in a 25 mph zone, but because no houses existed on that road Holman believed it was against state law. Was that why, Grossman asked, you think the Knox County judge is corrupt? Holman: "Why can't he clear him? . . . I think that is a corrupt thing to do."

Was it true, Grossman asked, that Holman had refused to accept his son's high school diploma, had torn it up, and had called the school principal and superintendent corrupt? Holman denied tearing up the diploma and calling them corrupt, but he had accused them of being "unjust and un-American." At another point, Holman asserted that the newspapers had published many "lies" about him.

Holman also had complained that Fisheries Department wardens had failed to protect him from having lobsters stolen. During 1956, or possibly 1955, he claimed to have seen two men hauling his traps and named them both. One of them was Walt Teal, who he thought had died recently. Grossman asked a young man in the courtroom to step forward, Bertram Teal (Walt Teal's nephew), and asked Holman if Walt Teal had not been dead for four or five years. Holman thought it must be two years. Did he know that when he died Walt Teal was seventy-two years old? Did he know that for approximately five or ten years before his death "his hands were very crippled, is that right?" "They weren't crippled, but—he could row an oar to beat the band."

Where was Holman's church? Port Clyde. How many were in his parish? "How many . . . ? The whole community, the whole world, wherever I can reach them." He estimated that seventeen attended the service last Sunday. When was he last pastor of a church in a building designated as a church? Nineteen years ago, when he resigned with a unanimous vote to stay. From 60 to 120 people came to his house with tears in their eyes, begging him to stay.

At one point Grossman invited Holman to go to the blackboard to mark another spot and then sat down, giving him the floor. Galgay: "Your Honor, I hate to discommode my brother, but I think there is some intention meant by his seating himself when this witness is about to answer." Later on, Grossman drew out Holman on the subjects of why the MLA was wrong and his love of the flag and our government, "the most beautiful institution that ever graced God's Universe . . . the most wonderful Government, I'll fight for it etc., etc." And after the judge intervened again, Galgay quipped: "I think the reporter may need some Band-Aids for her fingers at this point." Grossman: "And you won't let me sit."

As the afternoon wore on, Galgay objected to Grossman's latitudinous questions: "I think we're learning that unless this witness is asked specific questions, that Pandora's box seems to have opened up and there's no end to an answer." The role reversal seemed to have been complete when after another intervention Grossman kindly offered, "I don't wish to interrupt *my witness*." He did get Holman to repeat his mantra that "the Government of Canada, for Canada, and by Canada shall not perish from the State of Maine." Grossman: "And is that what you believe [Maine's representatives] have stood for?" Holman: "If you had thirty-one years of it, you'd—yes, yes." Pressing further: "And you believe that as honestly and sincerely as all your testimony?" "I believe it just as sincerely as I can believe it."

The shooting incident, to which Grossman always returned, had occurred while Holman was in his boat not far from the wharf and while a young man—a seventeen-year-old, Neal Hupper—was shooting, said Holman, at birds. But then Holman had jumped in the air when he felt a bullet whiz by his left ear and heard the young man say, "Tee-hee." Pressed by Grossman, Holman changed his line from an attempt on his life to: "I think he shot to intimidate me." Grossman, however, *eventually* pointed out that Holman had subsequently given Neal Hupper a ride in his car and had not mentioned the incident. He also had not spoken to the boy's father about it, though he said he knew him well.

All this testimony continued to be interspersed with Holman's claims to be fishing for "the rights of the individual citizen of my government" or "the Admiralty law of the United States" and the like. At the end of the day, Judge Gignoux for one had heard enough. He met with counsel in chambers and requested them to get Holman off the stand as expeditiously as possible.

Accordingly, the following morning, on May 28, Grossman moved along briskly and with more limited questions. He established that Holman had reported the shooting incident to the Sheriff's Office but filed no charges. Was it possible, he asked, that the boy accidently fired near him? "Not a ghost of a show in God's Universe." Did he not tell the newspapers, because of this incident, that "Chicago gangster tactics are being used" by the MLA? No.

Grossman then revealed that the Huppers, father and son, were not members of the MLA. He also introduced as evidence a letter that Holman had written to the Rockland *Courier-Gazette* (published August 15, 1957) protesting that he had had nothing to do with the Justice Department lawyers coming to Maine. His letter professed ignorance of antitrust laws and issues, thus contradicting his earlier courtroom testimony that he had studied antitrust law "for years" and opposed the MLA for that reason. "Minimum price was not even mentioned," he had written. (The letter also noted that Holman's dory had disappeared briefly during the tie-up, apparently hidden for a couple of nights by other fishermen, then returned to the water. Neither Galgay nor Grossman questioned him about this.) With a parting salvo that Holman had never heard anyone except his own son threaten the life of anyone ("a lie," Holman shot back), Grossman finally, to everyone's relief, ended his cross-examination. Galgay did not hesitate to excuse the witness.

The government next called, to the disbelief of some of his neighbors, Mr. Stacy Prior, who could have been a model for a portrait labeled *Maine Gothic*. A tall, gaunt old man who looked all his seventy-six years (and who was said to have always "looked old") lumbered to the stand after the fisherman sitting next to him nudged him hard and directed him to go forward. Asked his name by Joe Nowlin, Prior replied: "You'll have to come up [so I can hear]." Nowlin: "Your honor, this witness is a little hard of hearing. I will have to speak loud and slow to him and may have to get closer than I normally would." Again he asked for the name. "My name?" "Yes, sir." He gave it and then spelled it on request. "And where do you live?" "Huh?" "Where do you live?" "Medomak." The judge: "The Court is going to ask that the witness speak as loudly as he can." "Huh?" Gignoux patiently asked Prior to try to speak to the back row of the jury: "Can you hear me?" "I'm sorry, I'm awful deaf but I can't help it."

Nowlin then painfully established that Mr. Prior was a fisherman who last summer fished for lobsters in the Medomak River area, hauling just sixty to seventy traps from a "common row dory." He had used an outboard motor but "she burned out, and I couldn't use 'er." When Nowlin finally got the witness to hear his question regarding anyone trying to stop him from fishing last summer, Prior expanded: "There were three fellas. Afta' I et my dinnah', I went off to haul. I hauled one trap an' I see this boat comin', it come up along—not alongside of me but just a little distance. He says to me, 'You throw that trap overboard.' I says, 'I'll throw that trap overboard when I bait it.' I baited it an' throwed it overboard. I rowed to the second one an' hauled that one. Then he come alongside of me, one of the fellas grabbed my painter...." Who were the three gentlemen? Verge Prior, Lester Teele, and Vernard Prior. "Well, afta' they took my painter, I went forward and I took my jackknife and I cut my own painter. Then one of them—I can't remember which one—grabbed ahold of my dory, got my dory and held me," and they towed him into the dock with their powerboat.

What else had happened? "Nothin'—I went ashore." Had he resisted? "Well . . ." Now Grossman objected, but here Prior's hearing improved and he injected, "Yes, sir; yes, sir," and as Grossman renewed his objection, "I had a right to do it." He could not remember which man grabbed his boat "because I was so worked up. I didn't notice hardly what was goin' on." Nowlin: "What did you do?" "Huh?" "Did you do anything?" "Yes, sir." "What?" "I throwed a rock aboard." By now the courtroom rocked with laughter. Nowlin: "What did you say, sir?" "I throwed one rock aboard the other boat." "What else did you do?" "Well, I can't remember doin' anythin' else. I thought that was enough." Were the three men members of the Maine Lobstermen's Association? "I'm not able to be here too long," Prior rasped, "because I'm not very well, I'm goin' to tell you that right now." Nowlin: "We'll let you go very soon." "My heart isn't too good," Prior wheezed, "I'm here to do the best I can for you."

"Are you a member of the Maine Lobstermen's Association?" continued Nowlin. "What's that?" "Are you a member of the Maine Lobstermen's Association?" "No sir. I was last year, until I give the card up to Millard Creamer. I'm all out of it. I won't join any more unions or anythin'. I'm too old a man, I'm retired now, I'm all done fishin'. I've sold my gear, dories and everythin'. I've done my hard day at work, and I'm all through." No further questions.

Grossman asked only three questions, revealing that the three men in the boat, two Priors and one Teele, were nephews of old Stacy Prior. Indeed, they made up only a small part of the Prior and Teele clans, most of whom had lived offshore on nearby Bremen Long Island until World War II. Many had then given up their independent, subsistence ways for good jobs generated by the wartime boom. Stacy Prior had run oxen on the island before the war, and coming to the mainland had not made him ambitious. He lobstered, clammed, fished, and lived in what shore people call a "camp," a two-room, ramshackle cabin not far from the Medomak town landing. After the judge said "You may step down," Stacy Prior departed with, "I ask for all Peace on Earth."

Stacy's nephew George Lester Teele, one of the men who grabbed the boat, testified next. A big, bulky man with large glasses, wavy hair, and an ever present cigar jammed pugnaciously between his teeth,

Lester Teele was known as a hard drinker. Most of the time, he wore tall clamming boots and, when he had the money, always stuck a pint of firewater inside one of them. He looked younger than his years all his life, they said, even to the day he drank himself to death. Lawyers questioning Lester on the witness stand or chatting outside the courtroom easily picked up the scent of alcohol.

Lester Teele fished throughout the year, seining and clamming when not lobstering in the summer. He owned a twenty-two-foot powerboat and fished 75 to 100 traps. Asked if he was a member of the MLA, he replied feistily: "I have been right along, but I think this is the end of it." Nowlin asked him the usual questions regarding meetings and the MLA. Asked who were some of the men at a meeting, Teele named two, stopped, and said: "I could go on for a week." Asked again, he replied: "I've told you two. I guess that's plenty."

Teele fended off questions from Nowlin with vagueness and an instinctive thickheadedness, but then went too far. Asked about the substance of an MLA meeting, he replied: "I'd rather not discuss it." Judge Gignoux firmly told him he was required by law to answer and that his wishes did not matter. Teele then admitted that the local MLA delegate, Millard Creamer, "says to stay ashore until we get 35 cents, but I don't think they set no price."

Nowlin wanted to know what happened when Teele went out to bring in Stacy Prior (as well as Teele's own father, who was eighty years old). Teele said of his uncle Stacy, "We took aholt of his boat, and he was mad," but put up no fight. "Well, he throwed one [rock], I think, in the boat." This prompted Nowlin to approach the bench and say that Teele be declared a hostile witness and that he be allowed to cross-examine him. He wanted especially to reveal "a rather colorful incident."

During the bench conference Grossman of course objected to Teele's being declared hostile, and raised the issue of the government attorney having talked to Teele improperly three weeks before. Gignoux said that they would discuss the latter in chambers at 1:15 P.M., then quickly ruled that Teele was a "hostile and reluctant witness"— the fifth declared so far—and so informed the jury.

Now Nowlin zeroed in on what else Stacy Prior had done to resist being towed. "Do you recall . . . testifying that your uncle struck your brother-in-law, Verge Prior?" "With an oar." Chuckles through the room. Nowlin: "Tell us more about it?" "He just struck him with an oar." "One of the dory's oars?" "It would be one of his dory's oars." More laughter. "Did he hit him hard?" "Well, hard enough," said Teele with obvious disdain for the landlubber, "it wouldn't feel very good, would it?" Even the judge was smiling by now.

Grossman got Teele to characterize the incident as "a little family matter," but Nowlin returned to get an admission from Teele that the group that went out to get his father was no family group. Further, he asked if Millard Creamer had ever said to him, "Whose got the guts to go out and bring in old man Teele?" And Lester said that he answered, "I got plenty."

Grossman responded by playing on the theme of the poor, scared fisherman intimidated by government men, and by bringing up again the encounter in Rockland three weeks before. Was Lester scared? "No, I am never scared." Was he disturbed by the government men? "Well, I don't like to be in a crowd like this. What I mean, I ain't used to it." But the prosecution again deflected Grossman's thrust by getting Teele to admit that when Nowlin went to his uncle's house, Teele had spoken to Nowlin of his own accord. With a grunt, Lester Teele then departed the witness stand.

The lawyers, however, continued to discuss Mr. Teele. At 1:15, in chambers, Grossman presented a new wrinkle and sought to use the Medomak fisherman as the basis for a motion to declare a mistrial. He complained that Joe Nowlin had spoken to Teele in Rockland while his client was "visibly intoxicated," on the same day Nowlin had refused to speak with him while sober. Grossman claimed that testimony was thereby introduced into the case and that the defendants had been defamed and injured by this evidence. Nowlin replied that he believed that "the rather spectacular occurrences in the lobby of the [Thorndike Hotel]" early in May had been arranged in advance—by Grossman, he implied. He then repeated that he had assured any fishermen present that they had no obligation to speak to him. He had so told Teele at his uncle's home. To be sure, "he appears to smell of alcoholic beverages every time I have ever seen him," but he was not in disorder and he spoke intelligibly. "He says he has asthma and has to drink all the time," and what he said was in substantial agreement with what he told the grand jury last August. Clearly Nowlin resented Grossman's suggestion that he had acted improperly.

Judge Gignoux seemed bemused and said that even if all that Grossman said were true, it would not be grounds for a mistrial. As it was, then, he saw no evidence of improper conduct by any counsel. He also thought that inquiry into Lester Teele's drinking or his state of intoxication at any time was irrelevant. Grossman could inquire, if he wished, as to Teele's state that very morning, or as to whether he were constantly intoxicated, but the court did not wish him to inquire regarding Teele's condition at the times Grossman had discussed. Grossman eventually decided to cork the matter of Lester Teele and his bottle.

Next to come to the stand was Verge Steven Prior, of the oar. This fifty-one-year-old fisherman was of medium height and very rugged. With long, graying hair, a round, blunt face, and wearing a bright plaid shirt, he looked like a longshoreman. His answers to Nowlin's questions were clipped and mostly direct, at least until he came to the subject of an MLA meeting in Medomak. "Well, I heard a few down there talking. That's the only meeting I've been to." He did recall that about twenty-five fishermen got together and that Millard Creamer, "the head member" of the MLA, "just asked me if I'd knock off and wait for the price of 35 cents." Everybody agreed to stop fishing except the two old men (he referred to Lester's father as Ira Dell).

Verge Prior then claimed with a straight face that he asked Stacy Prior to stop fishing "just for the fun of it." When Nowlin got to the oar, Verge dissembled again: "Oh, he just thrashed around with an oar, that's all. I guess he just played a little, hit me two or three times." "Hit you with what?" "Oar, one of his oars." "Did he do anything else?" "Well, I think he throwed a rock in my boat."

Once again Grossman characterized the incident as a family affair, "fooling around," to which Verge Prior readily agreed. "And your uncle didn't hit you with the oar so that it bothered you, did it?" "Naw, it didn't bother me," said Verge smiling broadly, "I wouldn't have cared if he hit me over the head," and the room erupted with laughter.

From Muscongus Bay the prosecution shifted its attention again to Casco Bay. Now Philip Bloom (the young, kosher New Yorker who could barely stand the sight of lobsters) questioned a witness. Frank Moon, a South Portland lobsterman in his sixties, had been a member of the MLA but now bore a grudge against the organization—or at least against Bay militants. He came to the courthouse wearing a fedora, and with his rimmed glasses, arched eyebrows, and loud sports shirt he looked more like a retired store clerk. But Moon was a tough loner who dared to work the Portland ship channels, thereby exposing his gear to the hazards of passing vessels and sometimes fierce competitors. Moon had tied up for nine days during the first stoppage. During the second, however, he asked MLA Vice-President Rodney Cushing if he could "move some traps." Cushing, he said, "refused me permission to go" because the rest of the fishermen opposed it. "What happened after that?" "I had to drag up a hundred and fifty traps." "Will you explain what 'drag up' means, sir?" "Well, that's tow a grapple along the bottom and catch the lines." Moon claimed that this cost him approximately a week's work and that he was unable to recover ten traps. Though less helpful to Bloom in discussing MLA activities, Moon did confirm that Les Dyer "presided" at the Harris Company roof meeting and that the fishermen agreed on 35 cents.

Alan Grossman asked Moon if it was not a fact that during 1956, 1957, and even 1958 lobster fishermen who had traps in the Portland ship channel lost them when ships came in and out. "Not a hundred and fifty in ten days, no." "But you have lost traps there before?" Yes. "And you have had to grapple there?" Yes. "And losing traps in a ship channel is not that unusual?" "That's right, no, it ain't." "And when you stopped fishing you stopped as an individual and not as a member of an organization?" "That's true." With that, Frank Moon left the stand, and a fifteen-minute recess ensued (2:40 to 2:55 P.M.) because the next witness would be on the stand for a long time. As Rodney Cushing came forward, reporters crowded in to listen to the questioning of the MLA vice-president.

The handsome Cushing, dressed in a dark-blue suit, tie, and white shoes, looked more like a vacationing sportsman than he did a lobster fisherman. But this Cliff Islander, though he lived part of the year in Portland, could be characterized as a "highliner." "I have," he said, "an 18-foot open boat, 5-foot beam, with a 35 horsepower Johnson motor and a 2½ horsepower Briggs & Stratton motor. I run approximately three hundred traps in the height of the fishing season, the rest of the season about two hundred." He estimated he caught about twenty-five thousand pounds in 1957 for a gross income of $7,300. Associated with the MLA from its founding in 1954, Cushing had joined the Executive Council in 1955 and was elected vice-president in 1956. His answers to Joe Nowlin's questions were usually clear and direct, though sometimes, because he liked to talk and explain, they ran on a bit.

Cushing recalled dates with ease and, though loyal to Dyer and the MLA, gave the impression of being a cooperative rather than a hostile witness. Ever the diplomat, Cushing implied that he had nothing to hide and wanted to help everyone understand.

News reports of the trial led with Cushing's assertion that the fishermen stayed ashore during the second tie-up because they "had the impression" that Governor Edmund Muskie (because of his suggestion of a mediation committee to Les Dyer) wanted the fishermen to stay ashore. This came shortly before adjournment and, despite the fact that Cushing admitted he had no direct oral or written communication from the governor to that effect, the newspapers were full of it. However, other parts of Cushing's testimony were more important.

After contradicting Frank Moon's story of their conversations about moving traps during the tie-up (his recollection was different: "I had no authority to give him permission or non-permission to do anything"), Cushing launched into a long narrative that ended by implicitly laying the responsibility for the tie-ups at the doorstep of the dealers and their broken promises. He had believed, he said, that the MLA and the Casco Bay dealers had an agreement—that "if lobsters became too plentiful and the dealers were plagued with lobsters, that they would so inform me and that I would go to the fishermen and ask them to slow down for a day or two. . . . [T]hen suddenly on a Monday night the word came down to me from Mr. Willard, President of the Willard-Daggett Lobster Company, that lobsters were going to drop to 30 cents a pound." After the word spread, "there was not a boat hauling traps . . . everybody was tied up because they knew they could not fish for 30 cents." The fishermen on Cliff Island "felt they were willing to stay ashore until 'H. froze over five times around.'"

Cushing admitted that he favored staying ashore until the price rose, but denied that he had a set price in mind. In fact, he asserted, he feared a specific price, "not for the fear of violating antitrust laws but [because] in the fall of 1956 we stayed ashore for approximately a week [when the price had dropped to 30 cents] . . . [and that after] we got 35 cents a pound . . . the Portland dealers told me in substance at a conference [that] if 35 cents a pound is what you want, 35 cents is what we will cram down your throats for the whole year, so I felt that any price ceiling [*sic*—he meant minimum] would be dangerous."

When shown the government exhibit of the MLA's meeting record, and after having read the sentence about the vote on a 35 cent minimum, Cushing disagreed with that "conception" of the meeting's outcome. A half-dozen prices were discussed, and he characterized what Nowlin called a "vote" as an "opinion poll." Similarly, when asked if delegates were given instructions as to what to report to their communities, he replied: "No, sir, no instructions. Mr. Dyer never gave anybody instructions nor neither did I. Absolutely not."

Cushing also told of speaking frequently during the tie-up with John Willard and Edward Palmer at Willard's office, "mostly with Mr. Willard." He could not recall any suggestions he might have made to Willard, however, though he remembered one of Willard's which he carried back to the men: that they go back fishing for ten days at 30 cents a pound. How was that received? When Cushing made that suggestion to the fishermen on the Harris Company roof, to MLA members and nonmembers, they all "turned [it] down flat. I thought they were going to throw me off the dock for suggesting it."

It was now the end of Wednesday afternoon, and the workweek was over. Judge Gignoux had ordered an early recess because of the Memorial Day weekend ahead. Before adjournment, Joe Nowlin, thinking of Cushing's adherence to arguments made by Alan Grossman (newspaper reports even referred erroneously to Cushing as a "defense witness"), requested the judge to admonish the witness not to discuss the case with counsel for either side. This was customary, said Nowlin, in several districts where he had practiced. Grossman, asked if he objected, bristled: "I have a resentment of it but no objection." Beaming at the jury, Gignoux asked them also not to discuss the case and wished them "a pleasant holiday and a pleasant weekend."

The Portland Waterfront, 1950s. Photo courtesy of Portland Telegram and Gazette.

Alan Grossman (left) and Leslie Dyer (right) Admiring New MLA Banner with Ote Lewis, Ash Point Lobsterman and MLA Public Relations Officer (center). Photo courtesy of Barry Faber.

Lobstermen Vote to Stay Ashore, August 7, 1957, at MLA Meeting, Rockland Community Building. An estimated six hundred fishermen attended the meeting during the height of the tie-up. Photo made from a photocopy of a picture appearing originally in Rockland Courier-Gazette.

Judge Gignoux, sometime in the 1960s. Photo courtesy of Portland Telegram and Gazette.

Fishermen's "Mug-up" Nets $450, February 22, 1958. This dinner was held at Owl's Head Central School auditorium to raise money for the MLA legal defense. Photo made from a photocopy of a picture appearing originally in Rockland Courier-Gazette.

Irene Manoogian Arabian, 1959. Photo courtesy of Irene Arabian.

Fisheries Experts David A. McKown (standing) and Louis Robert Cates, circa 1958. Photo courtesy of Charles L. Marr.

John J. Galgay (left) and "Star Witness" John T. Holman, May 27, 1958.
Photo made from a photocopy of a picture appearing originally in Portland
Press Herald, *courtesy of The Portland Newspapers.*

Left to right: *John Knight, Rodney Cushing, Leslie Dyer, and Alan Grossman at Courthouse. Photo courtesy of Barry Faber.*

Alger and Shirley Burgess, circa 1960. Photo courtesy of Shirley Burgess.

Myles "Mike" O'Reilly, August 1, 1957, during the Tie-up. Photo made from a photocopy of a picture appearing originally in Portland Press Herald, *courtesy of The Portland Newspapers.*

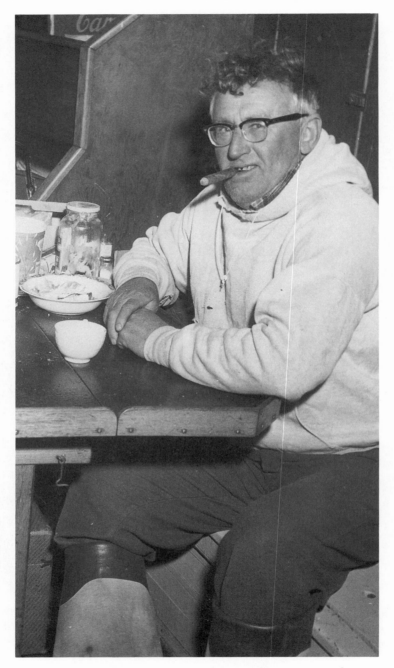

Lester Teele and Cigar, 1962, aboard the Sardine Boat Beverly Ann. *Photo courtesy of Everett Boutilier.*

Left to right: *Verge Prior, Lester Teele, and Uncle Stacy Prior, May 26, 1958, Waiting to Testify at Courthouse. Photo made from a photocopy of a picture appearing originally in Portland Press Herald, courtesy of The Portland Newspapers.*

Stacy Prior, circa 1960 in Front of His Two-Room Home at Medomak, Maine. Photo courtesy of Everett Boutilier.

Leslie Dyer's Lobster Boat, Used as Prop in 20th Century-Fox Film Deep Waters *(1947). Photo courtesy of Vinalhaven Historical Society.*

5   THE VERDICTS

"[W]hy is it that all these rugged, individualistic lobster
fishermen decided to tie up at the same time, all along
the coast from Kittery Point to Eastport?"

—*Joe Nowlin*

he following Monday, on June 2, 1958, Rodney Cushing arose
early as usual at his apartment in Portland. During the past
several months he and his family had been living in town
where his son attended high school. He had made coffee and had already picked up a newspaper at a nearby stand before breakfast. Then
he and his wife drove in their red 1955 Buick Skylark to the High Street
garage, and walked to the courthouse, arriving a good forty-five minutes early.

The reporters who had erroneously labeled Cushing a "defense
witness" inadvertently revealed just how effective he was for a defense
that was otherwise in trouble. There was nothing "hostile" about Cushing even as he parried the prosecution with a tone of reasonable disagreement. He was articulate, and his disarming willingness to give
information contrasted sharply with the defiant or evasive demeanor
of previous MLA loyalists. This held true even before Alan Grossman's cross-examination brazenly turned him into a virtual defense
witness, which Gignoux allowed over Galgay's protests. When he took

the stand again at 10 A.M., beginning the final week of the trial, Cushing held strong and steady despite Joe Nowlin's occasional sarcasms, and boosted the spirits of defense counsel and the fishermen.

Nowlin returned to Cushing's admission that he himself had received no direct communication from Governor Muskie indicating that the governor wanted the fishermen to stay tied up. From there he hammered again at the 35 cent price minimum. Cushing still refused to acknowledge that the MLA vote in Rockland had been targeted on 35 cents. Casco Bay's second tie-up ended, he said, because fishermen heard via television and radiotelephone that men in the central coast had gone back fishing. They resumed also because "it was an economic squeeze. . . . Those boys were heavily in debt. . . . They had to fish." Yes, there had been frequent cautions against any use of violence. Why was it necessary to warn so often against violence—because it was likely? No, said Cushing, but anytime a couple thousand men are involved there will be hotheads; he and Les Dyer thought violence was just a "faint possibility." Finally, was the MLA a cooperative for marketing lobsters? No. Nowlin had finished.

Grossman lost no time in raising issues dear to his heart. Were fishermen unable to buy bait from a dealer if they did not sell their lobsters to him? Didn't some MLA members complain that they must obey dealers to whom "they were in hock"? Didn't fishermen reveal that dealers who owned islands were insisting on 3 cents a pound tribute from fishermen who fished around those islands? Over prosecution objections, Grossman also offered an instance of fishermen going against an MLA "opinion poll." He asserted that a majority had wanted to retain a smaller Maine gauge rather than adopt the slightly larger Massachusetts measure, but then some MLA men lobbied the legislature on behalf of the latter.

Grossman plunged on, with Cushing uncharacteristically doing little talking. The MLA did not set a minimum price but left it to the officers to *negotiate* with the dealers. The tie-up had been encouraged by at least two Portland dealers who urged fishermen to slow down for a while. Nowlin finally interrupted, objecting that Grossman seemed to be testifying and Cushing merely assenting. But after slowing down momentarily and giving Cushing more time to answer, Grossman, as intense as ever, slipped back into the same pattern.

Judge Gignoux allowed Grossman a latitude that the Rockland lawyer exploited to show that the MLA had been reasonable, legal, and
willing to negotiate, while the dealers had been greedy and inflexible.
Gignoux finally reined in Grossman when he tried to discuss dealers'
meetings. After the noon recess, Grossman turned to the "isolated incidents of requesting fishermen to come in" which, Cushing agreed, had
never been authorized or sanctioned by the MLA. Did Cushing ever tell
any fisherman to tie up? Never. If Cushing had told a fisherman to tie
up, would he have? "No sir, he would tell me to go to 'h.'" And hadn't
it been the pride and joy of the Maine Lobstermen's Association that it
represented the rugged, individualistic fishermen along the coast of
Maine? "That's correct."

As soon as Grossman finished, Nowlin sprang to his feet for redirect examination, asking sarcastically: "Mr. Cushing, why is it that
all these rugged, individualistic lobster fishermen decided to tie up at
the same time, all along the coast from Kittery Point to Eastport?"
"Because they—my—" and now Cushing flushed and became a bit
heated: "You want my opinion of this?" Nowlin provocatively repeated the question and Cushing cut loose: "Because they felt at long
last somebody had the guts to stand up and fight and everybody was of
the same feeling, that this rock bottom price which had been imposed
on us was something that had to be combatted some time and now was
the best time to do it!"

"*Imposed on us.*" That was the defense's main redoubt, and the
jury had now heard it many times. Nowlin, of course, led Cushing back
to admissions that the tie-up's object had been to gain "a *better price,*"
and that in the absence of MLA action that past summer the price
would have fallen further, to 25 cents or lower. Grossman then returned to replay his themes. What besides fishermen tying up, he
asked, prevented the dealers from dropping the price? "Nothing else,"
other than the government's antitrust indictments against fishermen
and dealers. Then the government excused Cushing, easily the defense's best witness so far.

John Galgay, after a long absence because of his ulcerous stomach,
now returned to question a large, dark, and very nervous fisherman

from Long Island, Elliott Hall Ricker, known in Casco Bay as "Pood."
Ricker fished 230 traps from a twenty-foot open boat around the islands of Basket, Little Chebeague, Crapboard, and Long. His winters,
when he worked as a stationary engineer for the Maine Central Rail-
road, were perhaps more isolated than his summers.

The quiet Ricker, an MLA member, had attended a fishermen's
meeting at the VFW Hall on Long Island during the tie-up, but said:
"I didn't vote. I never voted to a meeting in my life what I attended."
He had swallowed his dissent, and later he had gone out and been
asked to come in. Galgay wanted all the particulars, but the lawyer's
dyspepsia worsened as he struggled with "Pood's" awkward shyness
and evasiveness. Galgay quickly lost patience: "You can't answer or
you won't answer?" He strode to the bench and requested that Ricker
be declared a hostile witness because he had previously testified quite
differently.

Grossman interceded, saying that "one of the dealers who has been
with us in this trial came to me this morning and informed me that
this man hasn't slept, hasn't eaten, he has been so upset at being sum-
moned as a witness, and the one that he was afraid of was me cross-
examining him, and I submit that I have never seen this man before in
my life." To declare him hostile, he pleaded, would be prejudicial to
the defense. The judge was "not satisfied that this witness is truly
hostile," so Galgay resumed and Ricker, in any event, became more
forthcoming.

Ricker described how he had been asked to come in during the first
tie-up. The Long Island delegate "came over to where I was haulin'. He
didn't come alongside of my boat, he came up within talkin' distance.
He said, 'My telephone's been ringin' all of the mornin' and the strike is
still on.' I finished my string of traps and come in."

Ricker also recalled a morning wharf gathering of the fishermen
on Long Island at which George Johnson had said, "I don't call it fair
for anybody to go out and haul their traps. We voted to stay ashore."
But Ricker replied, "I am goin' out and haul. You didn't see my hand
up to go ashore." Nevertheless, a second time Ricker was visited on
the water and he had come in. Willingly. Galgay: "Now when he visits you out on the water you meekly submit and refrain from fish-

ing?" Ricker saw it differently: "If I hadn't of [wanted to], I wouldn't have come."

Grossman, true to his word, asked Ricker no questions.

Raymond Leroy Hamilton of Chebeague Island had been on everyone's mind ever since Alger Burgess said that Hamilton told him he had broken ranks with other fishermen during the tie-up because his wife had nagged him into it. Indeed, Ray Hamilton might well have experienced difficulties with his first wife, since their stormy marriage would end a few years later in divorce. The truth also was that Hamilton had shunned the MLA, and enjoyed a cozy relationship (and perhaps a better price) with Jack Willard, to whom he was related.

At forty-seven Ray Hamilton, wearing a simple green sweater, cut a handsome figure, tall, with brownish-blond hair, blue eyes, and high cheekbones. He had started fishing at age twelve, "all kinds of fishing," like his father before him. (The elder Hamilton had also captained the *Nellie G* for a dozen years during the 1930s and 1940s—the trim, small ferryboat whose successor in 1958 still carried summer people to the island from Portland and Falmouth.) In the 1950s Ray spent two-thirds of the year lobstering, and the rest of the time did some kind of fishing. During the trial, he was seining for mackerel and living in Portland because his daughter was in her high school years. It was from his thirty-eight-foot lobster boat, however, that Hamilton fished some two hundred fifty traps and made most of his $7,800 gross income. (He enjoyed other fishing more, though, and liked the risk and planning it took. Lobsterfishing was not much of a gamble. But in either case, he liked being out on the water.)

In a slow, soft-spoken but clear drawl, Hamilton answered Alan Lewis's questions about the meeting of Chebeague Island fishermen at the parish hall of the Methodist church. He went along reluctantly with the decision to stop fishing ("I didn't want to but I would") and he tied up for more than seven days. His version of the encounter with Burgess was that not much was said either way, "but he did say that I ought to feel conscience-stricken for being out there, and I told him I did a little bit but I thought it's time I went back to work." After "the whole of them together" asked Hamilton to go in, he stopped fishing and went in. Lewis: "Why were you out fishing that day?" "For the very same reason everyone goes fishing: to make money."

Hamilton's independence surfaced testily as he sparred with Alan Grossman. "Do you put back into the water," asked Grossman, "half of what you take out." "No, sir." "Well, isn't that one of the lobstermen's rule of thumb, estimates of their income [sic]; that whatever you get out of the water, you usually put back half?" "Maybe some lobstermen's, but it isn't mine." He also thought that 30 cents "wasn't an unfair price to me," and he declined to say that he knew that others thought it unfair. Grossman retaliated by asking rather unkindly if he was "the gentleman whose wife insisted that [he] go fishing?" "If it is, I don't know anything about it." Grossman: "Do I understand that you did only what you wanted to do during July and August?" "Yes. . . . Nobody tells me to go fishing, [or] when I can't." Did Les Dyer ever tell him anything? "No, sir, I don't know the man."

Lewis returned briefly, however, to why Hamilton had stopped fishing. "I didn't want to go against all my friends and neighbors." Lewis: "Would you have stopped hauling if Mr. Burgess hadn't had this conversation with you out on the water?" "No, sir, I wouldn't." And Ray Hamilton was excused.

"Dyer Warned of Violence, Jury Is Told." Thus did the *Portland Press Herald* characterize the testimony of the day's last witness, a slight, bookish-looking young man who looked every bit the general science and chemistry teacher he now was in Scarborough. But for three years before, through the summer of 1957, John W. Morton had been a lobster fisherman. Originally from California, Morton graduated from Dartmouth College in 1950 and settled in Maine three years later. Morton had fished three hundred traps from a thirty-two-foot boat, and from his gross of $8,000 in 1957 he claimed a net of $3,000. Though no longer fishing, this clear, honest witness proudly owned that he still belonged to the MLA, and he stoutly defended Les Dyer and the fishermen.

Morton also consulted a daily record he had kept of the number of traps he had hauled and of the pounds of lobster taken during the previous year. So he knew exactly when he stopped hauling during the tie-ups and recalled fairly well the gist of what Dyer and others had said at the Harris Company rooftop meetings. Dyer had said unequivocally that the MLA did not condone "any sort of violence, and . . . that if any fisherman wanted to go out and fish, that was that individual's own business." Morton did not evade the key issue of price: Dyer had indeed recommended that they not fish for less than 35 cents.

Morton said that although he had voted with the minority to go back fishing at the third Harris Company meeting, in the end he did not do so and honored the majority decision. "So your course of action," Lewis asked, "was against your conviction?" "No, sir. . . . It didn't seem fair or sportsmanlike to me to go out and haul traps when there were fishermen staying ashore . . . as a matter of principle. . . . [M]any of the fishermen who were staying ashore could ill afford it, just as I could [not]."

Alan Grossman tapped this sympathetic witness's eloquence to drive home the point regarding fishermen's independence, but Lewis retorted once again by asking why these individualists had all tied up at the same time? Because they could not make a living "catching 30- and 32-cent lobsters." So the day ended with Morton echoing Cushing's argument that the price cut had precipitated the tie-ups by preventing fishermen from making a living wage.

Tuesday, June 3, began with uneventful, somewhat repetitious testimony from three lobstercatchers, all of whom had broken ranks during the tie-ups. Two were names made known to the court by John Holman: the Port Clyde men whose "visits" on the water he had seen, Howard Simmons and Clayton J. Pease. The third was Evans Lloyd Doughty of Cape Elizabeth, a Casco Bay fisherman who had figured prominently in news reports of the second tie-up as a dissenter.

Simmons, another member of the exodus from Bremen Long Island, was forty-four years old, slender, dark and shy, and had fished since he was eighteen. His testimony consisted mostly of a litany of "I don't remember's," along with "I can't give no dates." Pease, also in his forties, wore a work shirt and a worried look to the stand, and had been an MLA member who attended one fishermen's meeting at the Martinsville Grange Hall. "They just asked me in a nice way if I would come in," he said, and when asked if the meeting's vote had been for 35 cents, replied: "It was." Cross-examined by Grossman, he offered no relief to the defense, but he did tell the government lawyer Philip Bloom (in another rare appearance before the court) that he did not really want to stop fishing, "but I felt I had to stick with the fishermen."

The courtroom stirred with more interest as Evans Doughty took the stand. Tall and thin, with sharp rawboned features crowned by clear glasses, the fiftyish "Ev" Doughty was an impressive-looking man. With his thirty-six-foot boat he fished 170 traps in the winter and 250 in the summer, and sold his catch to Willard-Daggett. His gross income of $9,923 signaled that he was a highliner, and his testimony suggested a good relationship with Jack Willard, despite the fact that he had been an MLA member in 1957 (but was no longer). He had agreed with the first tie-up, he said, and stayed ashore. During the second, however, he went fishing. It was Doughty who had threatened at one of the stormy Harris Company rooftop meetings that if anything happened to his gear, he would "go through the association" and "there wouldn't be a buoy left in the whole ocean."

Now Doughty testified about an implied threat to him during the second tie-up. He had come in to the wharf in Portland, and Rodney Cushing came over and asked him if he would stop hauling for a couple of days because, Cushing told him, "the boys at the island was gettin' kind of irritated" and, according to Doughty, "I don't know how long I can hold them." Doughty immediately softened the impact by adding, "Well, as much as to say keep them from hauling; I didn't know exactly what he meant by what he said." John Galgay, however, asked about another possible meaning: "Or were they ready to take off on you?" Doughty (as Grossman objected): "I wouldn't say that." But he had implied it.

Asked what price he was getting during the tie-up, Doughty was ambiguous, saying that he was getting 12 cents more for the hard-shell lobsters he was catching farther out on the water. Doughty was indeed a "great hand at fishin' outside," but he gave the impression that he sold his hard- and soft-shell lobsters together—unculled—for an average of "probably 37 cents a pound." (More likely, as a Willard loyalist, Doughty was simply getting paid more for his shedders. He never said exactly what he was paid for shedders.) Galgay: "Is that the reason you did not want to join this tie up?" "Not necessarily. . . . I didn't think I had gained anything from stopping the year before."

Strangely, Alan Grossman asked Doughty only one question, the motive of which remains a mystery. He asked if he was related to one Sanford Doughty (a Chebeague Islander), whom Ev identified as his cousin. Then Grossman let him go.

The government now called its final witness: appropriately, Elroy Johnson of Harpswell–Bailey Island, the model for the statues of the generic lobsterman. Six feet tall, well proportioned, with chiseled good looks, white hair, and eyeglasses, Johnson was an imposing physical presence. Johnson commanded respect among fishermen because he had been a deputy commissioner of the Department of Sea and Shore Fisheries and was an intelligent man with a deep voice and an aura of self-confidence. When he spoke, fishermen listened. During the summer, he ran a gang of four hundred traps, and fished year round. Though friendly with Les Dyer, his disagreement with Dyer during the tie-up was well known.

Joe Nowlin asked Johnson to repeat the gist of his dissent at the Harris Company. Clearly uncomfortable, Johnson eventually explained that "I thought it was a mistake, that I didn't see how we could win, and I did think we would lose." Why? "Well . . . two reasons. The first one and chief one . . . is because the Maritime Provinces, Newfoundland and Quebec province produce about two and one-half times the amount of the State of Maine and being victims as we are of our reciprocal trade agreements, our markets are wide open to that two and one-half times and any gap—" Nowlin: "Excuse me. Is that what you said at the meeting?" Johnson: "I don't remember." Continuing, as if he had just brushed away a fly: "Any gap that we would leave open in the field of distribution could and would be readily filled by the Canadian lobsters, so I didn't see how we could win." Nowlin quickly changed the subject to the price of lobsters.

Johnson admitted that he was paid 35 cents *during* the tie-up. He advocated that others fish at 30 cents, however, because of the timing ("the peak of production"); it was better to sell three hundred pounds at 30 cents than to wait and sell a hundred pounds at 40 cents. He was visited on the water, he said, by a group of men unknown to him and was asked, "Elroy, why won't you help us?" By his answer—"I think I am helping you"—he meant that he thought they should all go back to work.

Nowlin did not press Johnson for names and other details when his witness brusquely said he did not recall such things. When Nowlin did probe as to how long he tied up and when, Johnson grew irritated: "No, not to permanently tie it up. Now, have you that answer clear? I don't want to give confusing answers. I told you that I did tie up, as I promised, for the first period that the boys were out. . . . I didn't tie up for the second period. Now, does that clarify my answers?" "Yes, Mr. Johnson, that's perfectly clear. Now these people who came alongside you and asked you to stop, did they say—" "I don't remember saying that they asked me to stop, sir." "Well, asked you to help them. . . . did they say anything else?" "Probably. There was other conversation went on. What goes on between fishermen, we do what we term 'speaking each other,' go along and talk to each other any time, middle of the day, just ask: How's the children getting along, if his wife's well and so on, and then we resume work again."

When Nowlin returned again to the safer topic of price, Johnson grew vague, and added: "I like to get along with my neighbors, and plan to." But he conceded that his understanding of the tie-up was that "the boys felt they couldn't operate for less than 35 cents." With that, Nowlin finished. Again Grossman questioned the witness briefly, complimenting Johnson and touting the great respect in which he was held by other fishermen.

Moments later, the parade of witnesses ended. Galgay announced, "The Government rests its case, your Honor." The judge acknowledged Galgay, then turned to Grossman, who said: "May it please the Court, *the MLA and Leslie Dyer rest their case,* and we would like to discuss matters with the Court in Chambers."

There would be no defense witnesses, for they had already appeared. Most of the fishermen appearing as government witnesses had, under Grossman's cross-examination, served the defense. Now the judge dismissed the jury until 9:30 the next morning, with a caution not to form any conclusions until they had heard the closing arguments. He then retired with counsel to his chambers.

Inside, Alan Grossman immediately presented two motions of judgment for acquittal for Leslie Dyer and the MLA. He argued that the case should not be submitted to the jury because the government had not proved a conspiracy—indeed, that there was "not a shred of evidence that Leslie Dyer in any way conspired with any other individuals." The government, Grossman claimed, had not shown that all the Maine coast fishermen were involved. What about Vinalhaven, or Beals Island? The government's own witnesses testified repeatedly that they could fish or not fish, as they chose.

The first hint that a camaraderie had developed between the defendants and the government lawyers came to the surface when Grossman acknowledged that the government had been helpful to the entire lobster industry by its investigations, though he thought it "would be a crime" to label the Maine fishermen as criminals. He now detected sympathy from the government's attorneys: "I think when they came in to Court in the beginning, there was vim and vigor, . . . [but now] as an iceberg melts away, so they melt; and . . . we say that they do now understand our problem. I don't think the Government understood it before." Now they knew, said Grossman, that the MLA, its officers, and attorneys "left no stone undone not to combat their Government. . . . I think it's common knowledge amongst the Coast of Maine that the problem of the fishermen is one that's been existing from time immemorial, ever since dealers became dealers and fishermen were fishermen."

Joe Nowlin countered that the fishermen had acted together and that all the government needed to do was show concerted action for a "better price," whether specific or not. He said that Grossman himself had practically conceded there had been concerted action. Regarding the areas of Maine not treated, under the Sherman Act it is not necessary that such agreement cover 100 percent of the market. Even if there was evidence that the fishermen acted in response to an effort to impose a price, "that's obviously no defense in a Sherman Act case. In practically every price-fixing case since 1890, some such defense has been made. The defendant has always said: We had to do it, we were being driven to take a low price, the market conditions were disor-

derly. . . . [S]uch defenses are quite immaterial." Many witnesses admitted to the 35 cent minimum, others dodged it, but "the least any of
them said [was]: We wanted a better price." On the strength of the
MLA documents alone, "if the Government had introduced [them] and
rested then, this case should I think go to the Jury."

Following briefer exchanges between Grossman and Nowlin, the
judge rapidly agreed with the government. Indeed, he first said that the
evidence was sufficient "to sustain a conviction" of both defendants.
He then explained that he meant the evidence "is sufficient to submit
this case" to the jury without his expressing an opinion as to the verdict the jury might return.

Gignoux intended to deliver an instruction, or charge, to the jury of
thirty, possibly forty minutes, and he hoped that closing arguments
would be completed during the next morning session so that he could
submit by the afternoon session. Galgay suggested a maximum of two
hours for the government and said, "We'll try to keep it within an hour
and a half." Gignoux asked for a "genuine effort" to keep within an hour
and a half, adding that "after the first twenty minutes," counsel appreciated, "most of the effectiveness of argument has been lost anyway."
Grossman, too, promised to try to keep within the hour and a half.

Did the defense object to the government's using two counsel?
Grossman gallantly replied that "in view of brother Galgay's physical
condition . . . I think it would be perfectly agreeable to us that they
divide it up between whoever he wishes." Gignoux finally promised
not to interfere in oral argument unless it wandered far out of bounds.
Galgay: "That includes flags and cadets, I gather." Gignoux: "Right,
and music."

The tune the next morning in chambers was mournful for the defense, as Judge Gignoux accepted seven government requests as to instruction of the jury, with two minor qualifications, and rejected seven
defense requests. Then, shortly after 9:15 A.M., John Galgay stood before the jury, notes in hand, and summarized the government's case.

Galgay spoke slowly and distinctly, almost pedagogically, warm-
ing gradually and adding emphasis as he went along. He began with an
assertion that he had fulfilled his promise to show that there had been

an "agreement [he did not use the word 'conspiracy'] to stop hauling lobsters last summer for the purpose of raising the selling price to 35 cents." What the public wanted to know from the jury, said Galgay, was "whether you have come to believe, on the basis of what you have seen and heard in this courtroom, that Maine Lobstermen's Association and Leslie Dyer, along with hundreds of lobstermen who are not individually on trial as Defendants, agreed to tamper with lobster prices and to interrupt the normal and usual flow of lobsters from fishermen to dealers to consumers throughout the United States."

Like a professor giving a lecture, he enumerated several considerations that the jury must *not* consider. They must not decide whether the Sherman Act was a good or a bad law: since 1890 it had been "our settled economic policy" endorsed by Republicans and Democrats alike. It was not "some kind of newfangled legislation whereby you are being called upon to experiment with the desirability of its enforcement." The jury must not, in addition, consider whether the price fixed was good or bad, or whether the agreement was successful or not. Further, the question of punishment should not influence them.

Above all, the fact that the defendants may claim to have acted defensively, "resisting some other price-fixing conspiracy," should not be a factor. The governor's role was irrelevant: "Even if the Governor had authorized or condoned the actions taken by the Defendants, it would not relieve them of liability."

Galgay then turned methodically to those things the jury must look for. He quoted from, and commented on, five key documents, including one in Dyer's own handwriting. Regarding the witnesses, particularly the seven delegates of the MLA, Galgay cautioned the jury that it was not his memory or that of Mr. Grossman "that controls . . . but it is rather your memory of what they said that controls." Further: "Everyone that testified about these tie-ups stated that the purpose of tying up was to increase the price paid to lobstermen for their lobsters." It was difficult for anyone to believe, he said, that over two thousand MLA members all ceased to haul their traps at the same time based on independent, unilateral judgment. "That would indeed be a remarkable coincidence."

After reviewing the instances of patrolling and enforcement of the tie-ups, Galgay attacked the distinction drawn by Grossman and vari-

ous witnesses between votes and opinion polls. "You will recall the
testimony of the Vice President, Cushing, in this regard, when, on one
of the 102 instances in which he responded, within a period of 50
minutes, to statements made by my brother Grossman 'that is right,'
'that is correct' or some other similar, laconic, affirmative answer, that
the matters acted upon at these meetings were done so by opinion
polls." Galgay then recalled Robert Waddle's admission that the first
time he had heard that term was when Mr. Grossman used it here in
this courtroom. "You will also recall," Galgay said as he continued to
deconstruct Grossman's presentation, "that thereafter the words 'opinion polls' were included in many of brother Grossman's questions to
each witness who attended these meetings and these witnesses oblig-
ingly adopted the phrase as he coined it."

In his closing remarks, Galgay dealt superbly with the MLA's principal line of defense. He realized that the jury had heard "that lobster
fishermen had a hard time bargaining with lobster dealers." Nodding
his head, Galgay affirmed: "I think that testimony is wholly correct.
The only question is: 'What did the fishermen have a legal right to do to
overcome that evil?' " Waddle, he said, had done something construc-
tive and organized a cooperative. But the MLA had acted illegally. "I
predict that the Court is going to tell you that elimination of a competitive evil is not a legal justification for price fixing. . . . [T]he mere fact
that they had such a serious problem with lobster dealers is no justification for their price-fixing activities and you must, in conscience,
return a verdict of guilty." Lobster dealers in Portland, the jury had
heard, had been indicted for price-fixing. "But that is a problem for
another day and another jury."

You would hear eloquent protestations, Galgay continued, that the
defendants must have a fair trial. So, too, must the government. Listen
carefully to the Judge's instructions and apply whatever he says the
law is. Thus Galgay concluded as he began, with an appeal to the jury's
head and to the law.

Alan Grossman's concluding remarks contrasted sharply with Galgay's in substance and style. He spoke from no notes, calling attention
to that fact, and roamed the courtroom with animation and passion,
now facing the jury, then wheeling and addressing the government
lawyers, or turning and opening his arms and speaking to the fisher-

men out front. Though seeming to ramble, he hammered hard at several themes and unabashedly took advantage of what he himself called, using a sports analogy, his "home court advantage." Remarking often on the support and advice he had received from many prominent citizens around the state, he asked the jury: "Don't you know that the eyes of Maine are upon you?" He told the jury, in case they had missed it in news reports, that the defense team was getting no money. And he contrasted this with the cold professionalism of the outsiders from New York and Boston (even as he referred kindly to Joe Nowlin as "the Arkansas traveler, my dear friend").

If Galgay had lectured to the jury's head, Grossman went flat out for its heart. How could they, he asked, stigmatize the brave fishermen of Maine with the "badge" of "conspirators," men like Bob Waddle and Alger Burgess who had almost sacrificed their lives for their country during the war. Lobster fishermen were not big companies like Standard Oil, United Fruit, or Socony Vacuum Oil. The Sherman Act had never been intended to be applied to them. What "evil" had the fishermen done? They had resisted a price imposed upon them, on which they could not make a living, and so tied up their boats and put their lobsters "in a bank—God's bank, the bank of the Atlantic Ocean."

The government had asked the jury, Grossman said in a tone of disbelief, to disregard the governor, the state's senators and congressmen, and all the local defenders of "these conspirators." The prosecution had asked the jury to accept that what these defenders say "don't mean a thing. We are the attorneys for the United States Government. The king can do no wrong." A lawyer like himself, from the little shire town of Rockland, did not, like the government men, specialize in antitrust law "day and night." But the government had gone wrong from the start by bringing this case. Casting himself in the role of a local David against the outside Goliath, Grossman drew attention also to the "seven Government attorneys," including District Attorney Peter Mills, sitting in a phalanx of dark suits opposite him.

Recalling implicitly the melodramatic tears of John Holman, Grossman confided that he had been advised to be dramatic also: "Oh, yes, I could be dramatic with you; cry, why it wouldn't take too much to cry because inwardly in me my heart is crying because I can look back when the minister who is the First Vice President of this Association came to my office in 1954, Mr. Lenfesty, who is an ordained minister, came to my office with four of his brother fishermen . . . and said, 'Will you help the lobster fishermen in the State of Maine?' " No greater honor had ever been paid him, Grossman intoned, than to represent "these conspirators . . . these evil-doers . . . these people who violate the laws of their country by refusing to work at a cost below living."

The Maine lobster was a renowned delicacy; but, Grossman asked the jury, when you bought lobsters in a store or restaurant, "Did you ever think that these gentlemen [Burgess, Waddle, Johnson, etc.] were getting 30 cents a pound for those lobsters? And the Government says you should have fished for . . . 30 cents a pound. You should not resist the dealer. The fact that the dealer who was the cause of all this is himself indicted, erase that from your minds."

Turning then to notes he had taken while Galgay had spoken, Grossman asked why the government had not produced John Holman Jr., that "eminent young man who threatened to shoot others." Why, for that matter, he wondered with heavy irony, had Galgay given short shrift to "their star witness," the Reverend Holman? "He is the one you have been reading about in the papers . . . whose [sic] been over the T.V. and radio." But in his own county, where he lived, stressed Grossman, they were not really sure who or what the Reverend Holman was.

Grossman then characterized the government's handling of its fishermen witnesses as having "brother testify against a brother; hav[ing] a mother testify against its child." Rather implausibly, he praised the fishermen for not hiding behind the Fifth Amendment and for having nothing to hide. He was proud of his MLA clients, all honest men, and especially Les Dyer, "a dear and close friend of mine, a man who shared the same office with me for the last four years." But now the government wanted Leslie Dyer, Elroy Johnson, and Rodney Cushing to "wear the badge" of the conspirator.

Having tugged relentlessly on the jury's heartstrings, Grossman now paused and injected a note of humor as he returned to his David versus Goliath motif. It was a moment that all the counsel associated with the case would recall and relish for the rest of their lives. Once again Grossman used a sports metaphor, a reference to a famous group of football linemen.

"You know when the Government first came here if you notice how

strong these *seven stalwart blocks of granite* appeared. [Laughter] How
sure, how sure they were because they looked over to us and what did
they see? . . . They look[ed over] and they [said], 'Well, here is a bunch
of . . .' I hope they said— 'clean cut young men,' and included me in
that, 'who are going to try to do battle with . . . giants. We who have
prosecuted Morgan; we who have prosecuted General Motors, United
Fruit, and Socony Vacuum. . . ." Grossman hoped that he and his
colleagues had dispelled some of the government men's—though he
did not use the word—*disdain.* "I tried with every ounce of my energy
to come up somewhere in your eyes so that you would not look down
upon me [as you evidently did when you first came here]. You know
you were doing a job . . . and with you it is cold. How would you like to
be in my boots and each one of you I bet would, because it isn't pay that
we are getting, it isn't that we are cold, that we read from a paper. . . . We
talk to you from the heart. We have got more." Grossman evoked fishermen, Maine, a way of life; the jury's down-home common sense.

(Years later Peter Mills recalled John Holman's tears and Grossman's reference to "seven blocks of granite" as the most memorable
moments of the trial. Referring to the lawyers, Mills cackled, "These
were big, fat-assed guys," and Grossman was capitalizing on his under-
dog role as he delighted even the targets of his humor.)

The government, Grossman charged, had tried to put words in the
mouths of the fishermen regarding the famous 35 cents. But the fishermen told the truth and, yes, they did experience difficulty remember-
ing specifics of meetings. Who would not, he asked, unless blessed
with the phenomenal recall that Holman claimed to possess? The government also tried to make fun of the "rugged, individualistic" lobstermen, "and how far did they get?" Turning to the government squad, he
continued, almost fatherly: "You know, you don't know the lobster
fishermen. They are the most independent businessmen in the State of
Maine. . . . They don't look for any subsidies. They don't look for any
handouts." Moreover, in asking for divine guidance before all their
meetings, as the government exhibits showed, the fishermen were
clearly "God fearing individuals."

Grossman had tried many cases, but "I have never argued a case
this way in my life. You know it's just like being in the ball park, a
home ball park. Everyone in the stands is for you. Can I fail? My cit-

izens of Maine say that I shall not fail in defending a righteous cause because if my cause was not righteous, the citizens of Maine would not be behind us." Finally, and briefly, he offered a generous introduction of Stanley Tupper, and an appreciation of the fairness of "the distinguished gentleman who sits there as the Judge in this Court."

Stanley Tupper then rose to make a brief plea for the innocence of Les Dyer, "admittedly a deep friend of mine." Tall, boyish, and with a crew cut, Tupper spoke in low-key contrast to Grossman, sincerely and with a down-home charm. He described Dyer as a man who had assumed leadership whenever lobstermen faced a crisis. "Often his was the role of a peacemaker coming between the many varied factions in our fishing industry. . . . If each of you knew this man personally as I do, you would know how incongruous it is to think that this mild-mannered man would do anything to coerce anyone to do anything against his will."

Not only had the government failed to prove its case, said Tupper, but the evidence showed otherwise. During 1957 individual lobstermen were dissatisfied with the price. Supply far exceeded demand. Dealers wanted fishermen to slow down. "What could be more natural with the price of lobsters facing an all-time low in recent years and prices of bait, materials, boats and everything facing a record all-time high that they should congregate to discuss these common problems? These meetings served as a means for lobstermen to let off steam and if all groups of businessmen in this country did the same thing, there would [a friendly jab at Galgay] be no ulcers."

It had been conclusively shown that the votes or polls so much discussed by government attorneys were not binding on anyone, nor were they meant to be. Lobstermen of course made their own decisions. "This alleged conspiracy is a fairy tale. There was merely a common understanding by a majority of fishermen." Referring to his four years as commissioner of sea and shore fisheries and a dozen years working with fishermen as a lawyer, Tupper told the jury that if they found "this devout mariner" guilty of a crime, they would discourage leadership in the fishing industry for a decade at least. "This would be a staggering blow to Maine's third largest industry. I urge you; indeed I beseech you; I implore you to bring in a verdict of not guilty for the defendant Les Dyer. Thank you."

It was now 11:50 A.M. and Judge Gignoux called for a ten-minute recess after which the government would be allowed twenty minutes for rebuttal.

Listening to Joe Nowlin's rebuttal, members of the jury might have associated him with the character of Police Detective Joe Friday (played by the actor Jack Webb) on a popular television series of the 1950s, *Dragnet.* Joe Friday's mantra was "the facts, ma'am, just the facts." Nowlin said he would try to bring everyone down from the "stratospheric heights" of defense eloquence to "the facts." "You may have observed that in approximately an hour and fifteen minutes of argument, there was little attention given to the actual evidence before you in this case."

In reply to Grossman's complaint that the young Holman and others were not brought in to verify incidents of patrolling, Nowlin argued that enough time had been taken, and quipped: "We don't want to be here all summer. I don't suppose either the Jury or the Court or defense counsel would like that. The Rules of Evidence in the practice are a tribute to the shortness of life. You can't spend forever trying a case."

Though a tone of sarcasm at times crept into his voice, Nowlin couched his argument as a levelheaded appeal to reason. Grossman, he suggested, was simply asking the jury to disregard both logic and the plain truth of what witnesses and the documents showed. How could it be, he asked, that Mr. Dyer presided at a meeting and "took his pencil and his pen and wrote a false account of what happened and then put it in his files? Now, does that make sense?"

Regarding the witnesses, Nowlin paid particular attention to Elroy Johnson, "a man that defense counsel assures us ought to be believed." He (and others) testified clearly about being asked to come in and about the 35 cent price.

Judge Gignoux interrupted to tell Nowlin he had one minute. Three sentences later, the last of which mentioned "the facts" twice, Nowlin and the government finished, and the court recessed for a midday break at 12:20 P.M. At 2 o'clock, the judge delivered his instructions to the jury.

Always attentive to decorum, Gignoux thanked counsel for the "courtesy and respect" they had shown to one another and to him. To the jury he explained carefully and quite clearly (he would have made a superb law school professor) that his statement of the law was "controlling upon you" in applying the law and reaching a verdict, but that judgment on the facts "is your exclusive prerogative." He repeated what he had said at the outset of the trial about the indictment constituting only a charge and not evidence of guilt—thus they must begin with a presumption of innocence. The burden of proof for guilt lay upon the government, beyond any reasonable question. "This does not mean that you must be convinced of the Defendant's guilt to an absolute certainty, but . . . that you must be persuaded of the Defendant's guilt as you would want to be persuaded about the most important concerns of your life."

His discussion of the substantive law strongly echoed Galgay's concluding argument, and this was not lost on the jury. In explaining the law's meaning with regard to the term "conspiracy," Gignoux implicitly deflated Grossman's appeal to the jury not to stigmatize the defendants with a "badge" of shame. Conspiracy may be defined, he said, "as a 'combination' or 'agreement' among two or more persons to accomplish an unlawful purpose or act." He rephrased substantially all of Galgay's points, including of course the one that knocked down the defense's main redoubt: "It would not be a defense that the Defendants may have acted defensively to resist another price-fixing agreement among the dealers." Alan Grossman felt his "home-court advantage" slipping steadily away as the judge defined price-fixing in a way that seemed to fit exactly what the MLA had done.

After completing his instructions regarding the law, Gignoux told the jury that finally they needed to decide "whether the tie-up of the lobster fishermen along the Maine Coast last summer was the result of a mutual agreement or understanding . . . to refrain from hauling their traps until a better price for their lobsters could be obtained; or whether that tie-up represented individual actions by the fishermen resulting from decisions independently arrived at by each individual concerned."

Gignoux then urged the jury to use its own "good sense" in assessing the credibility of witnesses, and warned them not to construe any actions or words of his to indicate guilt or innocence, since he intended no such signal to them—the decision as to the truth was exclusively theirs. Gignoux had consumed just twenty-eight of the forty minutes he had allotted himself.

In a brief conference at the bench, counsel took no exception to the judge's charge, and then Gignoux told the jury how to handle the written forms of the verdict. Since it was a criminal trial, he said, the jury would now stay together until completing its deliberations. With that he graciously excused the alternates, and the jury retired at 2:40 P.M., Wednesday, June 4.

At 4 P.M. Mike O'Reilly left the courthouse and walked three blocks down to the waterfront, commenting, "The jury's got it and we done the best we could." Standing by his boat, the *Mary L. Louise,* O'Reilly told a Boston reporter that "it's time to get back to work." O'Reilly and his sternman were headed for the mouth of Casco Bay for another night of mackerel fishing. The night before, they had caught only sixteen mackerel and some sharks that tore their gill nets. "But the night you stay home," said O'Reilly, "is the night you'd have made a haul. So you don't stay home unless it's blowin' a gale."

At 5:25 P.M. the jury returned to the courtroom and asked the judge to repeat his instructions referring to Leslie Dyer. Gignoux briefly did so, and five minutes later the jury retired again. At 6 P.M. the jury left the building and enjoyed a quick lobster dinner at the nearby Falmouth Hotel, returning about an hour later.

After some four hours of deliberation, at 7:50 P.M., the jury returned with its verdicts. The clerk inquired: "Now, Mr. Foreman, what say you, is the defendant Maine Lobstermen's Association guilty or not guilty of the offense of which it stands indicted?" In a clear voice, Orlando Woodman replied firmly: "We have found the Maine Lobstermen's Association guilty." Then the same question for Leslie Dyer. And Woodman, firm but clipped and with a hint of regret: "Guilty." Grossman and his associates sat stolidly, controlling their disbelief and dismay. Les Dyer sat with his chin cupped in his hand, staring straight ahead. The government platoon maintained decorum, but sat erect and satisfied.

After the papers were passed, Grossman requested that the jury be polled individually. So the clerk called the roll and each juror replied yes.

Gignoux then ordered bail for Dyer fixed at $1,000 and directed that he be released on his own recognizance. The judge thanked the jury, assuring them that "you have performed your duties as American citizens in the highest measure." Les Dyer, after rising for recognizance and being told of his obligations by the clerk, uttered the only words thus far to issue formally from the man who had been so much at the center of these proceedings: "All right." Court adjourned at 8 o'clock. Sentencing would come on June 10, the following Tuesday.

The verdicts stunned most observers. Despite the "inland jury," despite the government having a strong case and the defense virtually none, most observers believed that a Maine jury would give Grossman a "home-court advantage." George Dixon, a syndicated columnist for King newspapers, had predicted that the government's case "will be blown out of court higher than a nor'easter." Even when the jury had come in at 5:30 with its request regarding Leslie Dyer, it seemed that if they convicted the MLA, they surely would absolve its highly sympathetic president.

Willis J. King, a twenty-nine-year-old public schoolteacher of history and of emotionally disturbed children from the town of West Poland, had served on the jury. He recalled years later with great clarity that his sympathies did indeed lie with the fishermen. But given the charge of the judge, the jury concluded without much difficulty (though with regret) that it must find the defendants guilty. "We hated like hell to do it," said Willis, but "we had taken an oath" and felt obliged to do our duty. Further, they shared the impression—intimated by both Galgay and Gignoux—that a correct verdict in this case was a step toward nailing the dealers, who most of the jury agreed were really at fault. Above all, Judge Gignoux had led them clearly to the verdicts.

Outside the courthouse Les Dyer and Rodney Cushing, both wearing suits, white shirts, and bow ties, stood talking to a reporter, hands thrust in their pockets. Cushing looked worried, Dyer pensive. Fishermen and their wives were leaving, uncomprehending and bitter. John Galgay stood by grandly enjoying his victory: "With all the fishermen I've met and seen, I can't dislike one of them. There was a law violated and anytime you work on a case the way we did you want to win it."

Dyer and Grossman's hometown paper, the Rockland *Courier-Gazette* responded with a full-page headline: "Lobstermen, Dyer

Found Guilty, Verdict of Federal Court Jury Stuns People of the Coast; Attorneys for MLA Exploring Avenues of Appeal." The paper predicted that "the series of bean suppers and fishermen's mug-ups that began last March" would be renewed, perhaps with more intensity. Though the defense lawyers worked for free and some of the witness fees wound up in the MLA's defense fund, the MLA was broke—and money would be needed for a continued fight. In an editorial, the same newspaper angrily berated the government's "questionable" victory and blamed the "whole mess" on those dealers "who saw fit to complain to the federal authorities . . . last summer." The government now needed, it said, to help a "distressed industry" that above all needed higher tariffs or restrictions on imports of fish and lobsters from foreign lands. In contrast, the Portland *Press Herald* defended the government's actions ("the law is the law") and recommended that fishermen turn to marketing cooperatives for a remedy.

Later in the evening of the dual verdict, the two court reporters, Harry Derry and Irene Manoogian, went to the Eastland Hotel, where the government lawyers were staying, to drop off—as one of them usually had—a copy of that court day's transcript. As they entered the lobby, they met Alan Lewis, who cheerfully urged them to come up to John Galgay's room to join the government team for a victory party. Irene readily accepted and Harry nervously agreed to accompany her. Derry's mouth dropped open in astonishment when a smiling Les Dyer, pipe and glass in hand, opened the door to Galgay's suite. The defense group had already joined the federal lawyers, drinking, laughing, and trading stories. Derry found it difficult to relax, and soon left, but Irene, doted on by the all-male group, smoothly entered the spirit of conviviality.

At the trial's start, the opposing lawyers had been testy with one another, but gradually they developed a mutual respect and camaraderie nurtured by their shared sympathy for the fishermen and by the experience of this unique antitrust trial. Dyer and his yarns, of course, pleased everyone, and how could the government men not like a man who had come over to them one day and said: "I can't believe it. Here you are trying to put me in jail. And yet you make me proud to be an American." That night the liquor flowed freely until most of the group went out to dinner.

The court reconvened at 4 P.M. the following Tuesday, on June 10. The day before, summer had been in the air, with the year's warmest day at a high of seventy-six degrees; but while fair skies prevailed, the temperature had now fallen into the fifties with a high of sixty. Defense counsel had filed a motion for acquittal and, failing that, for a new trial. Their arguments were heard promptly, with Grossman's young assistant John Knight speaking for the defendants.

Knight, his small crew-cut head bobbing with emphasis, returned to Grossman's earlier argument that the government's reading to witnesses of parts of their grand jury testimony had prejudiced the case. Further, the jury's request—during its deliberations—for a rereading of the judge's charge relating to Dyer showed that they had entertained reasonable doubt at least regarding the MLA's president.

Galgay brushed aside the use of the grand jury testimony, repeating that the government "had an abundance of the same kind of evidence through documents" already admitted. On the point that the jury's request had shown reasonable doubt, "I fail to follow that logic." It could have meant anything.

The exchange took barely fifteen minutes. The judge said he would rule after a brief recess, and did so at 4:25 P.M.

Gignoux as expected denied both motions, recalling that an identical motion had been presented in chambers on May 27. Use of grand jury testimony had been approved by the U.S. Supreme Court, and he echoed Galgay's point that Knight's inference from the jury's request was without basis. Then he asked counsel if they were ready for disposition of the case. They were.

John Galgay now enjoyed his most satisfying moment. His ulcerous stomach had never felt better since he had arrived in Portland. Confidently, oozing charm, Galgay dispensed justice and mercy. Because of the public scrutiny given to this trial, he did not want to create the impression that an infraction of the antitrust laws was trivial by recommending a trivial disposition. On the other hand, "I want it understood that I do not appear here today to demand a pound of flesh from the Maine Lobstermen's Association and Leslie Dyer. . . . I would also like to dispel the notion that the Government attorneys who presented the case were blocks of granite without feeling or understanding as characterized by my brother in his closing argument."

He believed that the defendants had learned their lesson and had "suffered humiliation by having 12 of their neighbors say to them: 'You were wrong for taking the law into your own hands.' " His investigation of the financial capacity of the defendants indicated that they were "practically without funds."

"I shrink from the prospect," he continued playfully, "of another series of mug-ups and bean suppers to raise the money to pay fines recommended by a vindictive and merciless prosecutor." He preferred bean suppers and mug-ups where lobstermen met to discuss ways of attacking their problems without price-fixing.

Therefore: "I recommend that this Court impose a fine of $5,000 against the Defendant Maine Lobstermen's Association and a fine of $1,000 against the Defendant Leslie Dyer. *I also recommend that both of these fines be remitted.*" A gasp like a cheer came from the twenty or so fishermen and their wives in attendance, and broad smiles crossed the faces of Grossman and Knight. A squaring of shoulders among Galgay's colleagues. "Of course," Galgay continued in a sober tone, "if the defendants should ever again violate the antitrust laws, on conviction the recommendation for punishment naturally would be much more drastic." If the court followed these recommendations, he finished, "I believe that such a disposition would truly be justice tempered with mercy."

A thank-you and benign countenance from the judge. Before imposing sentence, did the defendants have anything to say? As usual, Alan Grossman was not at a loss for words.

In a gush of thanks to five former blocks of granite ("no finer five gentlemen ever represented the United States Government") Grossman declared that his was no momentary conversion, but that Galgay & Co. had been "very gracious to us" during the trial itself. He saw good coming from the widespread publicity that the trial gave to fishermen's problems. Fishermen would indeed continue to hold bean suppers and mug-ups and to use the MLA and other legal means to attain a "fair living." He did not wish to quarrel with the jury, but the verdict "did shock the people of Maine." Yet because of the government's recommendations, "we say that goodness will come from this." So too would more cooperatives, "so that [fishermen] can stay within the law and certainly they are law abiding citizens . . . they are the rockbound coast of Maine. . . . [T]he lobster fishermen are the blocks of granite." If any fine imposed is remitted, "then mercy will be shown and justice will be done."

Alan Grossman knew well ahead of time what Galgay would recommend. Indeed, he had spent a good deal of the previous night arguing with Galgay over the amounts, pressing for smaller sums. At the end, it came down to a debate over the symbolic value of the size of the fines. This was the meaning of Galgay's statement that he did not want to give the impression of a "trivial disposition."

After inquiring if Grossman spoke also for Stanley Tupper, who was absent, Gignoux asked Leslie Dyer if he wished to say anything. Pleasantly, firmly, Dyer replied: "May it please the Court. I wish to state . . . that I appreciate the courtesies that we have received, and I want to personally thank the Antitrust lawyers whom we came to know and like, and I want to express our gratitude to our defense lawyers, Mr. Grossman and Mr. Knight, Mr. Tupper, Mr. Nixon and Mr. Chapman. I think that we have had a fair trial and am very happy to live in a country where we can have a fair trial."

Then, with a brief notice of "other proceedings pending before the Court which have not been finally disposed of" (the dealers' trials that had weighed so heavily in the minds of the jury), Judge Gignoux swiftly brought the trial to a close by imposing the fines and remitting each immediately. Adjournment. Handshakes, smiles, jokes, and laughter. Reporters would describe the final scene in the courtroom as a "love feast." Later, Les Dyer would send a "care package" of fresh lobsters to Galgay, and to each of the government lawyers a gift of MLA pennants, banners, and buttons.

EPILOGUE

Some parts of this story would never leave the fishermen's memories. Thirty years later, Alger Burgess and Mike O'Reilly sat together sipping beer and whiskey in a cottage on Cliff Island, reminiscing about the MLA and the trial. When a visitor asked a question, casually using the word "strike," they chorused: "It was a tie-up, not a strike!" But other parts of the story became hazy, and some just faded away.

As the years passed, recollection for some turned the whole affair into a victory for lobstermen. The dealers, after all, paid fines while Dyer and the MLA did not. The August after the trial, as lobstercatchers were hauling for good prices, five of the seven lobster dealers originally charged with price-fixing came before Gignoux for trial. Four of them changed their pleas from innocent to *nolo contendere* (no contest) and were fined: the Maine Lobster Company and the Benson Lobster Company paid fines of $500 each; the Willard-Daggett Co. and John E. Willard Jr. paid $1,000 and $250, respectively. The government discharged the fifth dealer—Charles E. Olson—because of "newly discovered evidence." (Earlier, in May, the E. C. Palmer Company and

Samuel L. Armstrong had pleaded *nolo* and drew fines of $750 and $500.) Years later, coastal folk recalling the trial usually exaggerated the amounts paid, especially by Willard. Even witnesses and their family members remembered fines of $10,000 or more for Willard.

What no one did recall was Gignoux's action concluding the Justice Department's civil suit against the MLA. Gignoux issued a permanent injunction against price-fixing and concerted hauling stoppages by the MLA, adding that nothing in his order prevented lobstermen from benefiting from the Fisheries Cooperative and Marketing Act of 1934. But the government had brought no civil suit against the dealers, so there was no permanent injunction against them. John Galgay gave the astounding explanation that the dealers' price-fixing agreement, unlike that of the MLA, had been made *only once* and covered a short period of time. In 1993 an interviewer asked Les Dyer's son Bert if the dealers had been price-fixing in the 1950s: "Hell, of course them dealers were price-fixin'. Everybody could plainly see it. Christ, every morning the dealers talk on the telephone and decide what the price is going to be. They still do."

Less than a month after the trial, the MLA, still feisty though reduced in numbers, held its annual meeting at Rockland and voted unanimously to form a cooperative. Meanwhile, the Maine legislature had passed a Fisheries Marketing Act (promoted by John Knight) putting cooperatives on a firmer basis. Yet despite this and the MLA's resolutions, by 1960 only two small, local cooperatives had joined three existing lobster co-ops for a total of five on the Maine coast. The commitment and capital for the MLA's proposal simply had not materialized.

What Alan Grossman and Leslie Dyer really wanted was an association that could bargain collectively on behalf of lobstermen. Maine's representatives in Washington during 1958–59 tried and failed to get federal legislation that would have allowed lobstermen to organize in the same manner as labor unions and farm associations. But the Sherman Antitrust Act, the jury's verdict, and Judge Gignoux's injunction blocked their path. The MLA, its teeth having been pulled, declined steadily, and lobster fishermen would never again manage to sustain the kind of unity they had in the summer of 1957.

Meanwhile, more men went out in faster, better-equipped boats and set more and more traps in Maine waters. From 1955 to 1965 catch-effort doubled as it had in the previous decade. In 1960 Les Dyer would marvel at nearly 1 million lobster pots, but that number would be dwarfed in turn by the multitudes to come. By the 1970s the slow-moving old-style winch used for hauling had been replaced by a hy-draulic hauler that made the process of drawing up pots both faster and safer. "This device more than any other," say the fishery's historians Kenneth Martin and Nathan Lipfert, "made possible the intensive fish-ing of the seventies and eighties." In 1974 the number of lobstermen rose to 10,523, and while lobster prices rose, they did not climb at the same pace as the cost of fishing. Rising overhead thereafter reduced the number of boats but still drove catch-effort frantically upward, seem-ingly with no limit in sight. In 1980, some 9,200 fishermen set just under 2 million traps.

Simultaneously a conservation lobby came into existence, based in the state Department of Marine Resources (DMR), the federal govern-ment, and university laboratories. By the late 1970s, scientists—known as "bug hunters" among the fishermen—warned repeatedly against overfishing lobster stocks, and pushed steadily for an increase in the minimum size of caught lobsters—set at three and three-sixteenth inches by the New England states. Fishermen—some called themselves "bug catchers"—were reluctant to accept increases in the minimum size, so the federal government began using the threat of further in-creases (in increments to three and a half inches) as a way to pressure the industry to adopt conservation measures.

Renewed concern for the resource led one fisherman to grapple with the "ghost trap" phenomenon. Loss of traps because of storms, errors, and cut lines was inevitable, and scientists began to tell the fishermen that these lost "ghost traps" continued to fish long after the bait was gone—for months and years—because lobsters also crawled into them seeking protective cover. The DMR scientist Robert L. Dow estimated that as many as six hundred thousand traps became ghost traps every year, and that they had a potential to kill up to 10 million lobsters annually. Cecil Pierce, who had begun lobstering in 1915 at age eight but went on to become a machinist, designed an escape vent that allowed snappers (undersize lobsters) to exit the trap parlor; legislation requiring vents took effect in 1979, though ghost traps continued to imprison lobsters of legal size.

A climate of unrelenting pressure to increase catch-effort actually led more fishermen to become receptive to the idea of trap limits and limited entry. Regulatory sentiment was stronger in Casco Bay than along the more traditional midcoast. Down East fishermen particularly disliked any law that would prevent their sons or semiretired relatives from getting a license. Yet support for trap limits continued to build, and in 1984 Swan's Island fishermen adopted a legislatively mandated program. Then Matinicus Island fishermen (in 1988) and Vinalhaven fishermen (in 1989) petitioned for local trap limits. Agreement on an ethic of limits, however, remained workable only locally.

In 1989, too, a major tie-up in Casco Bay showed just how far lobster fishermen were from the state of organization envisioned by Les Dyer and Alan Grossman, despite a degree of unity displayed by the lobstermen of Casco Bay not seen since 1957. Its outcome also left the structure of the industry and the fishermen's lack of leverage basically unchanged.

The episode—a tie-up that the news media almost uniformly labeled a "strike"—in part replayed the 1956–57 tie-ups, though without resulting in an antitrust trial. (Other tie-ups had erupted sporadically since 1957, including one in 1968 that again brought scrutiny, but no action from federal officials, and one as recently as 1988 involving some four hundred Down East fishermen.)

The 1989 tie-up idled a third of the coast for a week, including the great majority of lobstermen from the New Hampshire border east to the midcoast town of Friendship, on Muscongus Bay. What had happened thirty years before played little active part as guide or lesson, though, and barely existed as memory. Most participants were too young to know of the Great Lobster War. Some held dim boyhood memories; few seemed to think it relevant.

The cause of the 1989 tie-up, however, was basically the same as that of 1956–57: a sudden, precipitous drop in the lobster boat-price offered by dealers, coming after several years of overall decline. The average price for the first seven months of 1989 was $2.91, reflecting a sharp decline over the previous five years: 1984, $4.13; 1985, $3.97;

1986, $4.26; 1987, $3.23; 1988, $3.03. Meanwhile, the cost of bait, gear, insurance, fuel, and equipment had been rising.

At the end of July 1989 the shedders were running light in Casco Bay, and on Monday, July 31, four Portland wholesale dealers suddenly announced a 35 to 50 cent drop in price, down to $1.75 per pound. The last time the boat price had been that low was in 1981. Dealers blamed a glut of lobsters along with a downturn in Maine tourism. Lobstermen were stunned, and some immediately tied up their boats, insisting they would not fish for less than what they needed to meet costs.

At first it was knots of furious men spontaneously saying "Hell no, we won't fish." By Tuesday morning, a good deal of talking had taken place over boat radios and telephones, and fifty Casco Bay fishermen met at 6:30 A.M. on Widgery's Wharf in Portland and voted not to fish. (Where the Harris Company building had stood was now a black-asphalt parking lot.) A committee of three went to talk to dealers, and reported back that some dealers actually were encouraging a tie-up, because a slowdown in production would let them clear out their tanks. Meanwhile, more men were tying up and urging others to do the same. Throughout Wednesday more lobstermen in and beyond Casco Bay decided not to fish, including some who were getting $2.00 or slightly more.

Local newspapers and television and radio stations covered these events steadily throughout the week. Though fishermen's anger at dealers surfaced occasionally, it tended to be muted—in part because of a conscious effort by spokesmen to be diplomatic, and in part because the news media gave inordinate attention to fishermen who dissented from the tie-up or who were openly sympathetic to dealers. Billy Floyd, a forty-year veteran of lobstering, with stark-white hair, goatee, and a leprechaun face, told a reporter that "I can't see where [low prices] would benefit [dealers]. They've got their problems, too."

Most lobstermen agreed, though, that Canadian lobsters were a large part of their problem, and they blamed a big Nova Scotia catch then saturating U.S. markets. Casco Bay men had no other way of making sense of Portland dealers' talk of a "glut," because they simply were not catching many lobsters. Robert Waddle, the first government witness in 1958 to be declared "hostile," was now a small dealer operating on Pinkham Point in Harpswell. He agreed that Canadian lobsters contributed to low prices, but added: "There are too many people out there right now. The number of traps has gone way up . . . but the poundage has stayed the same." Edward Blackmore, the MLA president, on the other hand, said that Canadian lobsters were needed to keep both many dealers and many fishermen in business. Still, a scientist at the University of Maine conceded that, in fact, an unusually large surplus of Canadian lobsters was causing a stockpile of some 3 million pounds to enter the U.S. market later than it normally did. He called it "a little bit of a fluke."

Fishermen's meetings, we have seen, do not proceed by *Robert's Rules of Order*. At 6:30 A.M., on Thursday, August 3, 120 fishermen or more gathered at Widgery's Wharf in Portland to talk and to take another vote. No one called the meeting to order. The three representatives chosen to meet with dealers earlier in the week—all in their twenties or thirties—stood on the back of a pickup truck and just started talking to the men closest to them, and gradually the rest began to listen and to let one person speak at a time. Except for their sober faces, the congregated fishermen looked quite different from the photos of their counterparts in 1957. They were much younger and, not surprisingly, more hirsute, with mustaches, a few beards, and some long-hairs. They wore all kinds of casual garb, the plain work shirts of the 1950s replaced by T-shirts, tank tops, sweatshirts, cutaways, as well as sports shirts and slacks.

The committee perched on the pickup preached unity and suggested (not too strongly) that the men might want to stay in, stressing that a stoppage would allow the dealers to clean out their tanks. For the first half-hour or so, the men angrily supported staying ashore through the weekend and grumbled about low prices. Shortly after 7:00 A.M. dissenters began to speak up, and heated exchanges between them, the spokesmen, and other fishermen ensued. Impatient militants then called for a vote, and when asked "How many want to wait until Monday?" the men responded with a huge show of hands. In response to "How many don't?" only four or five hands went up, as at least two of the dissenters remained motionless. One of them, a well-known highliner and maverick, Albert "Skip" Werner, continued to protest the decision. Tie-up supporters reminded Werner that lobstermen down the coast who were getting $2.10 had already stopped fishing in support of the Portlanders. Finally, the meeting adjourned at ten of eight for an hour and a half: the committee would go talk to dealers and report back.

At 9:30 that morning the committee brought back little encouragement from the dealers. You'll get a higher price, they said, but we don't know when. Greg Griffin, the committee member who usually took the lead—smooth-faced, thirty-something, with the appearance of an office worker rather than of a fisherman—conceded: "I don't even play penny poker, and I'm up against men who make a living playing poker." After more debate and dissent, the meeting (their numbers fewer now) took another vote. It was as lopsided as before, in favor of the tie-up. At the docks, as some of the island men boarded their boats to return home, they heard that one of the big Portland dealers now was offering $2.25. They just shook their heads. "F— it. It doesn't matter, we're tied up 'til Monday."

The price of $2.25 did prevail on Monday and the lobster fleet returned to work. Dealers had given no assurances, of course, that the price would stay there. As Greg Griffin said, "That's called price fixing. We lobster fishermen expect fair market prices to prevail." The fishermen never did peg their actions to a particular price. The almost universal cry had been simply that $1.75 was too low.

In October, however, a chilling reminder of the past arrived in the mail for several lobstermen, including the head of a Boothbay cooperative. They had received letters from a Justice Department lawyer in New York City, asking for documents concerning lobster prices the previous summer and any agreements regarding price levels or efforts "to limit the supply of live lobsters for sale in Maine." Stanley Tupper, a former congressman and still a Rockland attorney, told a reporter that he had cautioned local lobstermen that summer against making statements suggesting they sought a specific price. It was one thing, said Tupper, not to go fishing because it did not pay. "The catch is when you try to set a price. That's technically a violation of antitrust laws." Referring to 1957–58, Tupper remarked: "Antitrust laws were designed to go after giant corporations. No one in their wildest dreams thought [the government] would go after lobstermen who were trying to get 35 cents a pound."

The August 1989 increase of 50 cents, however, hardly meant that fishermen had reached the promised land: $2.25 was well below the average boat prices of the late 1980s. As with earlier tie-ups, fishermen had talked much about the need for continuing communications and (Griffin: "I know it's a dirty word for many of us") *organization*. Most fishermen seemed to have accepted the situation, but a core group of some twenty-five Casco Bay lobstermen—with at least tacit agreement from another several dozen—hired a consultant (Alan Caron of the Waterfront Alliance in Portland) and soon launched the Maine Lobster Marketing Group (MLMG), whose principal goal was to find "a new marketing mechanism . . . to make sure the price [of lobsters] . . . is market-driven." Caron and the MLMG members frequently told reporters that they believed the dealers had not been honest with them during the recent tie-up. The strongest expression of this sentiment came in a Caron statement for the MLMG that most of the lobsters landed in Portland pass through the hands "of a handful of powerful lobster dealers. That is a condition ripe for mischief and manipulation."

The MLMG devoted itself initially to an intensive lobbying campaign to get lobsters accepted as a commodity by the Portland Fish Exchange. The Exchange, a publicly financed facility, had been in existence handling groundfish since 1986, offering fishermen a neutral place to display and sell their catch at an open market with open bidding, an assured honest weight, and guaranteed payment. Most wholesale dealers and buyers opposed inclusion of lobsters in the Exchange. Jeffrey Holden, owner of Coastal Fisheries, objected to the city-funded Exchange being used, as he and many dealers put it, to compete with private enterprise. Portland's daily newspaper, however, endorsed the idea in several editorials, noting that area groundfish dealers also had objected to the Exchange when it was first proposed.

The debate climaxed on October 25 when more than a hundred and fifty persons packed a room at city hall to testify before the directors of the Portland Fish Exchange. The past again linked with the present as the lobstermen advocates were joined by a white-haired, balding, spectacled, roundheaded fisherman from Cliff Island, Mike O'Reilly—as feisty as ever—and, after him, Alger Burgess's son, Ernie. A condition favoring the fishermen was that the Exchange had run in the red since its inception, and the directors (and city councillors) saw the addition of lobsters as a booster shot for the market. Accordingly, in December 1989 the board voted unanimously to admit lobsters. In the next few years, only a minority of lobstermen chose this route, but those who did were helped by the existence of bait sources other than dealers and also reported getting consistently higher prices for their catch. Lobstermen's use of the Exchange did seem to increase when dealers' prices dropped precipitously, suggesting that fishermen may have used it as a form of protest and as an alternative to not fishing.

Despite the 1989 show of unity among fishermen, the inclusion of lobsters in the Portland Fish Exchange, and the MLMG's successful and career-ending advocacy of the state-funded Maine Lobster Marketing Council, boat prices fell again in the summer of 1990, and in Casco Bay several lobstermen protested by donating barrels of lobsters to the elderly and the poor. "Individualism," manifested by intensified catch-effort and a lack of respect for boundaries and others' gear, escalated.

By 1993 the proliferation of traps in Casco Bay—now called the "Bay of Pigs" because of the wilderness of lobster buoys as well as the increase in unbridled rivalries infesting its waters—had led to trouble. With some strings growing to two and three dozen traps per line, tangling and cutting away a competitor's traps became rife. Lobstermen joked that the lobsters now lived in condominiums, with two and three traps of different fishermen sitting on top of one another. In Portland harbor, territorial conflicts had escalated so much in recent years that lobstermen had not only cut one another's trap lines, but had rammed boats, brandished guns, and thrown one another overboard. During 1993 an estimated five hundred traps were cut loose, worth an estimated $25,000. In early August of that year the state DMR intervened, imposing a ninety-day curfew which banned lobstermen from pulling traps between 4 P.M. and 6 A.M. in Portland harbor.

Meanwhile, warnings of overfishing and too much pressure on lobster stocks continued to be common along the entire Eastern coast, from Maine to Rhode Island and south. Federal officials continued their pressure to move the industry to a management plan that would include trap limits along with limited entry.

The government proposed that the minimum lobster size be moved up to three and a half inches in four steps ($\frac{1}{32}$ inch at a time) The threat of gauge increases (two of which had been implemented by the early nineties), pushed lobstermen to work with government representatives to develop a comprehensive conservation-management plan. The fishermen's cooperation with planning led to government rewards in the form of delays in planned gauge increases, and even promises of rescinding them.

Meanwhile, Maine fishermen landed staggering catches: in 1990 one of the highest of the century, 28.1 million pounds, to be followed in 1991 by the largest on record, 30.4 million pounds. The next year the catch dipped, but in 1993 it rebounded to 27.6 million, and in 1994 soared to the highest ever: 39 million pounds. "With the help of new technology," wrote one fisherman, "wire traps, lorans, big diesel engines, fiberglass, and synthetic ropes, we as an industry have become a very efficient catching machine." Many fishermen and scientists believed that the depletion of groundfish predators also made the crustaceans more abundant. Record landings did not deter the government from issuing repeated reports that lobsters were "overfished" and from warning that breed stock was in danger and that management plans must be moved along rapidly.

The immediate problem for fishermen, however, was the same old cycle: spiraling costs, stagnant price, and intensification of catch-effort. In 1990 the average price per pound fell to $2.21, climbing to $2.37 and $2.68 the next two years, but falling again in 1993 to $2.47, well below the most recent high of $2.81 in 1988.

The Great Lobster War of 1957–58 was a turning point for the lobster fishermen of Maine. They would never again strive for or attain the unity and leverage of 1956–57. The MLA would decline and revive, but never again focus on a minimum price. It would not, could not serve as an agent to bargain with dealers. It would continue as a meaningful organization and interest group, but would never again inspire the passionate loyalty of fishermen—especially those thoughtful farmers of the sea—as it had in the 1950s. During the 1989 tie-up most of the issues, arguments, and patterns of the 1950s recurred—and with the same conclusion for the fishermen.

By 1995–96 much had changed in the lobster fishery with respect to equipment, the men themselves (and sometimes the women), and even the unwritten rules of lobstering. A promise of escape from the effort escaltor was held out by proposals to establish a trap-limit law along with a moratorium on lobster fishing licenses. The initial legislation set 800 traps as a maximum, but would allow several years for fishermen who fished 1,200 or more to move down to 800. Although catches remained high in the mid-1990s (36.8 million pounds in 1995), most lobstermen favored some combination of trap limits *and* limited-entry into the fishery, thereby anticipating relief from pressure to increase traps and costs, less crowded waters and tangling of gear, and conservation of the resource.

Unfortunately, the reform fell victim to lobbying, legislative meddling, and Department of Marine Resources Commissioner Robin Alden's opposition to a licensing halt. The law's final version merely set a limit of 1,200 traps. Meanwhile, partly because of a rush to get into the fishery before a moratorium that was not to be, the number of license holders climbed from 5,557 in 1993 to some 7,700 by mid-1996. The relatively few fishermen who were reducing their gangs to 1,200 were more than offset by new fishermen and old who were now *building up* to 1,200 traps. The current president of the MLA, David Cousens of South Thomaston, lamented: "I used to love this job, now I hate it." Complaining of time consumed untangling gear, Cousens guessed that "we put 30 percent more traps in the water this year. . . . Every five feet there's a buoy, It's sickening."

Yet the image of the lobster fisherman as "rugged individualist" remained largely intact and promised to persist—even if slightly tarnished by unseemly episodes in the "Bay of Pigs." A romantic hue still colored the lobsterman's independent work in settings both scenic and dangerous. Except, however, for those relatively few fishermen who were members of cooperatives or who sold at the Portland Fish Exchange, the relationship of most Maine lobstercatchers to the dealers and to the market had not changed at all.

Acknowledgments and Sources

The sources for this book consist primarily of the trial transcript of *United States of America* v. *Maine Lobsterman's Association and Leslie C. Dyer* (United States District Court, District of Maine, Southern Division: Criminal Action no. 57-35) and interviews in person or by phone with most of the persons listed below. In addition, I used newspaper files, books, journals, and photograph collections in the Portland Public Library, the Maine Maritime Museum, and the Portland *Telegram and Gazette.* I also have benefited from reading *Commercial Fisheries News* for the past few years; its predecessor, the *Maine Coast Fisherman* of the 1950s, contained much information about the origins of the MLA, the tie-ups, and the trial.

A great many persons helped get this story told. It really started with Shirley Burgess who suggested—a long time ago—that I write such a book. If I had acted promptly, it would have been possible to talk to Les Dyer and several other individuals central to the story who were still alive. But I thank Shirley for the inspiration and for her friendship through Chebeague summers that now blend together for my children as they have for me over twenty-five years. Others who made special contributions to this project are marked with an asterisk in the list that follows, but John Chiquoine of Orr's Island, my father-in-law, must be mentioned as someone who at times virtually turned himself into a research assistant. Barry Faber, Alan Grossman's son-in-law and his successor as a lawyer and judge in Rockland, allowed me to see his copy of the trial transcript before I made my own, and helped arrange an illuminating and pleasant luncheon in Boothbay Harbor with Stan Tupper and John Knight. The latter gave me access to his scrapbooks, and the late George Putz let me look at Les Dyer's scrapbooks—and provided cheerful encouragement to tell the story. Raymond Gross hospitably opened the files of the Rockland *Courier-Gazette* for my inspection. Lou Ureneck gave me permission to use the photo morgue at the Portland *Telegram and Gazette.* Kelly Barber created the map and the illustration of lobstercatching gear. Thanks also to Paul Wright and Pam Wilkinson of the University of Massachusetts Press. Bob Putnam, a Chebeague Island lobstercatcher, let me look at his scrapbook relating to events in the 1980s and 1990s, and I learned much from conversations with him, and also with Ernie Burgess, and with Andrew Todd aboard *Old Salty.* Robert Levey, with his editor's eagle eye, read the entire manuscript in its final stages and scoured it for misspellings and other errors, as did copyeditor Charles Purrenhage. Neither they nor anyone else bears responsibility for those that remain.

Alley, Elmer C.
Arabian, Irene Manoogian*
Barnes, Donald
Bickford, Clyde
Bloom, Philip
Boutellier, Everett "Red"
Bowman, Sharon Burgess
Bracy, Irving E. Jr.
Brewer, Madeline
Brownell, William
Burgess, Alger*
Burgess, David
Burgess, Ernie

Burgess, Shirley*
Chiquoine, John*
Cushing, Rodney*
Davis, Sydney
Dooley, Dick
Dyer, Ada Mae
Dyer, Philip
Dyer, Victoria
Faber, Barry*
Galgay, Corinne
Galgay, Edward Gary
Gross, Raymond E.
Grossman, Constance Miller

Hamilton, Raymond
Heddericg, Steve
Johnson, Bernard
Johnson, George E. Jr.
King, Willis J.
Knight, John*
Lancaster, Ralph
Levey, Robert
Lewis, Alan L.
Look, Leonice Alley
MacVane, Donald A.
McConchie, Irving H.
McMasters, Barbara
McKown, David Arthur
Marr, Charles
Miller, Albion
Miller, Elizabeth
Miller, Ellsworth
Mills, Peter
Monaghan, Enid
Moss, Roy
O'Reilly, Myles
Palmer, Edward

Porter-Brown, Paige
Poulos, Richard E.
Putnam, Robert
Putz, George*
Roisman, Ann
Schaff, Ann
Sheldon, Karan
Simmons, Howard S.
Sparrow, Mary
Stimpson, Charlene
Todd, Andrew
Todd, Harold
Tonneson, Kenneth
Traynor, Sonny
Tupper, Stanley
Ureneck, Lou
Waddle, Robert
Weiss, David
Willard, Philip G.*
Willard, Philip G. Jr.
Woodman, Ken D.
Yocum, Kimberly

INDEX